Lakota Life After the Buffalo

Life and times of

Victor Swallow

Transcribed by

Vikki Swallow

Introduction, edited and arranged by

Gary W. Wietgrefe

Produced by GWW Books
Rapid City, South Dakota

GWW Books, 1811 Sunny Springs Dr., Rapid City, South Dakota 57702.
Website: www.RelatingtoAncients.com
Email: gwwbooks@outlook.com
Quantity orders: special discounts are available on quantity purchases by schools, book clubs, organizations, businesses, and others. Submit a request at www.RelatingtoAncients.com, or gwwbooks@outlook.com.
Print credits: Book production: GWW Books, Rapid City, SD.
Photos: Victor Swallow collection
Cover design by Gary W. Wietgrefe
Font: Garamond
Name: Swallow, Victor, 1939---, author.
Title: Lakota Life After the Buffalo
Subtitle: Life and Times of Victor Swallow

Identifiers: Paperback ISBN 979-8-9881736-7-0;

Subjects: Nonfiction: History
Classification: 1. LCO024000 Literary Collections/Native American;
2. HIS070000 History/Native American;
3. Regional Theme 4.0.1.4.11.0.0
North America/USA/States/South Dakota

First Edition. First Printing. Printed in United States of America.

Dedicated to remembering the Lakota transition since the late 1800s.

Contents

Editor Introduction

During a book signing at the Black Hills Farmers Market in Rapid City, South Dakota a local Lakotan, Victor Swallow, quizzed me about my book *Relating to Ancient Culture.*

A year later he came back and said, "I read your book about culture. I like the way you told about your grandfather." (My grandfather was born June 30, 1891 and lived with our family until he passed in 1976.) Victor, a half-generation older than I, never suggested he had written stories about his experiences.

In the summer of 2024, Victor, a well-poised, well-spoken Lakota arrived again with his youngest daughter, Vikki. As she searched for fresh vegetables, I quizzed Victor about his heritage. "I've written some stories about growing up Lakota. My mother's side was Hunkpapa; father's side was French. Our name was too hard to pronounce in French so the easiest way, we go by Swallow. Grandpa Swallow's mother was a Brule Lakota who left with Spotted Tail's band to Rosebud. Grandpa Swallow looked like a white man but would visit my mother in Lakota. Most of the stories I write about way back when are told to me by my mother Lizzie Two Bulls-Swallow." (See Chapters 4 and 8.)

Late fall 2024 I went to Victor's home and asked if I could put his stories in a book. He agreed....Gary W. Wietgrefe

Historical Background

South Dakota, well before history, was surmised to be a shallow inland sea. Eventually it dried and became flat grassland. Much, much later a series of glaciers moved south across the flat plains leaving occasional dirt ridges called moraines. For many years, the vast flat surface depressed under 1500 feet-thick glaciers.

Receding glaciers forced drainage south creating rivers. French fur traders entered waterways by canoe in the 1500-1600s. They moved west and south all the while trading and living with various Native Indian tribes.

Glacial moraines, in French "Coteau des Prairies" (hills of the prairies) were distractions as the traders fed on millions of grazing bison while they trapped furs on rivers and streams and traded with locals.

At first furs from the Plains were moved north along the Red River which separates what is now extreme northeast South Dakota, and the border between North Dakota and Minnesota. Eventually, a vast network of many Indian tribes supplied the Frenchmen with furs.

Frenchman, La Nouvelle-Orléans established New Orleans at the mouth of the Mississippi River in 1718. Fur traders used the Missouri and Mississippi Rivers and their tributaries to move the growing volume of furs south until 1800 when French Emperor, Napolean Bonaparte, sold Mississippi River drainage territory to the twenty-four-year old nation, the United States of America.

Throughout history diplomatic relationships have been sealed by marriage. The same happened in the Plains. Like other tribes, Lakota Indians sought new items, especially metal, brought by Frenchmen for trade. Naturally, native women married Frenchmen. Since Indian tribes did not discriminate against French trappers and traders, French/Indian children were unquestionably accepted.

Lakota offspring were eventually forced into the Great Sioux Reservation in 1868. With buffalo all but decimated, that is about when some of Victor's stories begin.

In 2025 Victor Swallow, part Lakota part French, lives as a retired, well-respected Lakota surrounded by family. This book tells how his family transitioned from the decimation of buffalo (American bison) to how his family gathers today to celebrate each other and life.

Lakota's provisional victory at Greasy Grass (a.k.a. Custer's Last Stand) into the twenty-first century, Victor is passing on oral stories from his mother, her mother's mother, and her mother's mother's mother.

As Victor ages, his mind and memory are sharp. His escape from Covid 19 death sparked more important memories he wanted to pass to his family and others. Thankfully, Victor's youngest daughter, Vikki, gathered his stories for me to arrange in this book.

This is important history the world needs to know….Gary W. Wietgrefe (editor and book producer).

Character Profile: Victor Swallow's Family

Family	Name	Born
Self	Victor Swallow	1939
Wife	Melidie Swallow	1942
Brother	John Swallow Jr.	1936
Mother	Lizzie Two Bulls-Swallow	1907
Father	John H. Swallow	1910
P. grandfather	Oliver Swallow	1870
P grandmother	Betty Beatrice Gillispie-Swallow	1879
P. great grandfather	Elias Swallow (Hilaire Soileau) B: St. Landry Parish, LA (French)	1843
P. great grandmother	Lizzie Iyotte-Swallow	1850s
P. great grandfather	David Talton Gillispie (an Irishman from Missouri)	1840s
P. great grandmother	Sara Long Jaw-Gillispie (she was a full blood Northern Cheyenne)	1850s
M. grandfather	Fred Two Bulls (Two Buffalo Bulls) (3/4 Lakota)	1870
M. grandmother	Mary Alice One Crow-Two Bulls	1871
M. great grandmother	Bird All Over (she was Fred Two Bulls mother)	1850s
M. great grandfather	One Crow (2 wives: Fannie & Rebecca)	1840s
M. great uncle Grandpa Jimmy	Jim Comes Again (Bear Comes Growling; (a.k.a. Kaakaa Jimmy)	1866
M. great grandmother	Fannie (married One Crow, then Joe White Plume)	1840s
M. great great aunt	Rebecca One Crow (a.k.a. Grandma Holy Day)	1840s
M. great great grandfather	Fire Heart (married Kind Heart) (both were Hunkpapa)	1820s

B= born, P = paternal, M = maternal

Victor Swallow's Genealogy

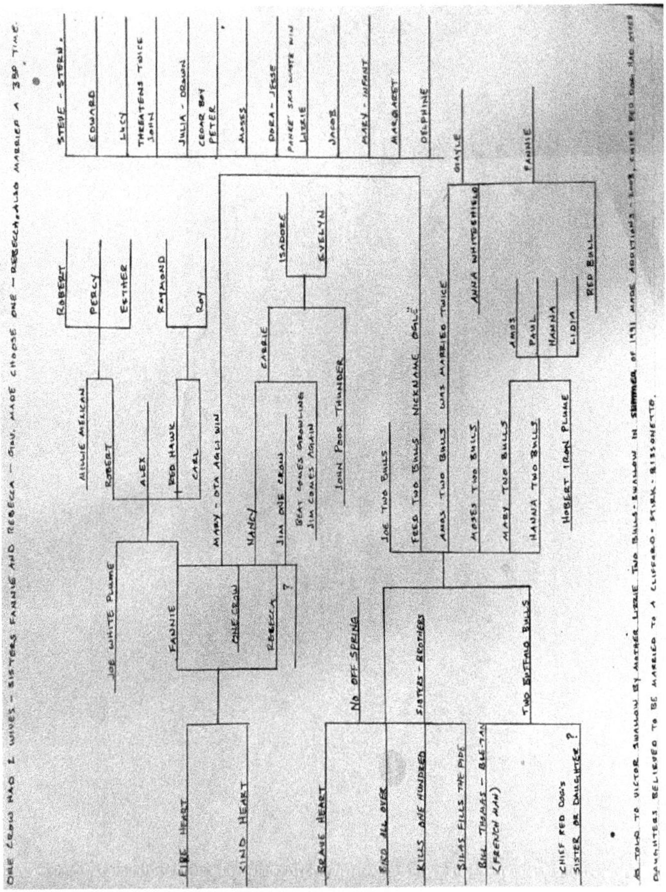

Top note: One Crow had two wives—sisters Fannie and Rebecca. The government made him choose one—Rebecca. After her death he married a third time and had a son, Jim.

Bottom note: This diagram as told to Victor Swallow by his mother, Lizzie Two Bulls-Swallow in the summer of 1991 with additions made in 2003. Chief Red Dog had other daughters believed to be married to a Clifford Stirk-Bissonette.

Family Photos

The three people confirmed at the Battle of Little Big Horn are: High Eagle (tall man center in hat), Joe Drags Rope (short man in back to right of High Eagle), and Comes Again (man very right end). Photo take 1935 or 1936-;about 50 years after the Battle when the three were young boys.

Joe White Plume and Fannie One Crow-White Plume, late 1800s.

Mary Alice One Crow-Two Bulls at Red Shirt Table, 1948-1949.

Victor Swallow's great grandmother Sara Long Jaw, and her daughter Emma Gillispie was born in 1893.

Bottom L-R: Victor Swallow's great grand-mother, Sara Long Jaw, and daughters Lizzie Gillispie, Magie Gillispie (Dreamer); Top: Emma Gillispie and husband John Flood. (Betty Beatrice Gillispie was older and not in photo.)

Fred Two Bulls (circa 1891) Brussels, Belgium with Buffalo Bill's Wild West show in Ghost Dancers Show. Fred Two Bulls as BIA policeman (circa 1900).

Hilaire Soileau (a.k.a. Elias Swallow) born in 1843, St. Landry Parish, Louisiana. Victor Swallow (2024) Oglala Sioux.

John Swallow family: mother Betty Beatrice holding Lizzie, Edna and John Swallow standing, Josephine in chair (circa 1920). Four generations: L-R Colin Swallow, John Swallow, Victor Swallow, Nathan Swallow (circa 2000).

Chapter 1

A story about a different kind of people

The many stories I could write about is of kindness, accomplishments or just people that impressed me but also people who are eccentric, a little odd, different or just a fixture in the Black Hills and Rapid City area.

In the 1950s and 1960s I have seen people over the years in the streets and around and never knew much about them but always seeing them around. I often wonder what kind of life they lead or what happened to them.

I remember there was a blind man who sat in front of JC Penneys store who played a fiddle with a donation container beside him.

And another lady who walked up and down the streets looking in the gutters. She was called Penny Annie someone said she had found some money at one time.

Another guy they called Pop Bottle and he picked pop bottles and when he ate he wouldn't touch any of his food with his hands. He would put his bread in a plate cut it with his fork and knife.

Another one was called Road Runner who walked up and down Main Street and St. Joseph Street never stopping.

There are many others and some are Lakota. The following story is about a lady who rode the streets of Custer dressed as a Lakota chief wearing a war bonnet with a little boy she called Little Beaver I believe. Tourist would pay her to have a picture taken of her or their picture taken with her. She wasn't Native but it was rumored she was married to a Native and her name was Mary Two Eagle.

I heard Mary had gone to the Deadwood Celebration at one time. She came to Red Shirt village on her way to Pine Ridge. She was leading a pack horse and had Little Beaver with her.

Red Shirt village is more than fifty miles from Custer and she had been seen in the Hot Springs area. No one I know knew who she was, where she came from, or even what happened to her. She was just there.

Somebody from Red Shirt told a story about Mary and Little Beaver riding somewhere and Little Beaver had a cotton rope he was playing with and got it entangled in the horses tail. The horse started bucking and threw Little Beaver off. Mary stayed on the horse and her war bonnet was moving back and forth while Little Beaver sat on the ground laughing at his mother.

The word was Mary got her horse under control and Little Beaver got a tuning for the cotton rope and laughing.

There are probably pictures of kids now in their 60s with Mary dressed up in a war bonnet from Custer.

These stories are a few of many different people who made an effort during tough times to take care of themselves.

As my generation slowly dies off unfortunately these people will be forgotten. I believe no matter how insignificant a person's life seems, each person should be remembered.

Chapter 2

A Lakota woman's bond with their child

The year has come and gone and the world is changing.

Our Federal Government, State Government and our Tribal Government are experiencing hatred and corruption to some degree but through it all I'm doing ok and at my age. OK is good enough.

I think back about the old times when Lakota women shared a bond with their children. As a man who has three of my own children, four grandchildren and six great grandchildren I still can't fully understand the bond between a woman and their child.

A woman carries their growing child in their womb for nine months. After delivering then nursing them they share a bond.

The following stories are about Lakota women who lived from the 1890s to the early 1920--my mother's generation.

All the Lakota women I knew loved their children. When seeing them nursing their babies always gave me a sense of calmness and that all is well.

The first Lakota woman that I will write about is Effie Rouillard-Two Bulls. She was my father's cousin. Their mothers were identical twins, Betty Beatrice and Jenny Gillispie.

Effie was married to my mother's brother Moses Two Bulls. Effie's oldest child was Fred and mom said he nursed till he was three years old.

Mom said one time she was sitting at the table and Fred was bothering his mother to nurse. His mother put cayenne pepper on her breast and let him nurse. He pulled away and pointed at the red pepper at his mother's breast. I guess he liked his milk spiked up.

The second Lakota woman I want to write about was my Aunt Dora Two Bulls-Fast Wolf. She nursed her boy Larry till he was four years old.

He would be playing outside with the other boys and he would say in Lakota, "Wait I'm going inside and get some ninny and I'll be back." He had sort of a puggy nose. It was said it came from all the ninny he got as a kid.

The third Lakota woman is my Aunt Jenny Marshall-Two Bulls who was married before she married mom's oldest brother Stern Two Bulls.

They had one child together, Alice Merle. Aunt Jenny was a mid-wife and she delivered my little sister in 1943 and my cousin Betty Two Bulls-Sanders. I don't know how many others she delivered.

Aunt Jenny had five children when she married Uncle Stern. When her oldest daughter died Aunt Jenny took her daughters two young sons and raised them as her own. Aunt Jenny was in her early 60s

In spite of her age, Aunt Jenny took on the responsibly of raising those grandchildren as many Lakota women did during that time.

She had a team and wagon that they hauled wood. One of the horses was broke to ride and they would saddle it and all three of them would ride into the badlands to look for agates to sell for a little extra money.

Aunt Jenny lived to be 95 years old and was born in 1891.

I am older now, tired, and worn out. Many times I think back to simpler times when Lakotans had family values, cared for their young, and took care of their elders.

I wonder how many of us Lakota with a conscience can look our ancestors in the eyes and say I am a Lakota with Lakota values.

Chapter 3

Life and Struggles in the Early Days of Red Shirt

The older I get I think back to my childhood when life was simple. We were grateful to get something to eat and were never picky about the food that was set in front of us.

We got our water from a well and had to carry it into the house. We didn't have indoor plumbing so walking outside during the winter to use the bathroom in an out-house was an everyday thing.

We got wood from nearby rivers and creeks and stockpiled it for the winter. We used the wood not only to heat the house but to cook over a cast iron stove.

At night we used kerosene lamps for lighting. We were satisfied with this simple life. That was all we knew.

Some families struggled with something to eat more than others but they all made it through to better times.

I want to tell their story, most I will not name.

I will start with my Grandfather Fred Two Bulls who moved to Red Shirt Table in 1900 and lived there till 1930 when he passed away at 60 years old.

Grandfather was a B.I.A. policeman. This story takes place around 1920 when at least seven of his eleven kids were at home.

From Red Shirt across the Cheyenne River to the West was a ranch. They had a ranch-hand living in a line shack who was a half-breed with the last name Lafferty. The shack was approximately 18 miles as the crow flies.

Lafferty stopped by and was visiting Grandpa Fred. Grandpa Fred invited him to eat with them. Mom said they had made a big pot of soup with big chunks of fat, onions and potatoes. Lafferty was thankful. He told Grandpa Fred that he has a whole shack full of food across the river and said to go help himself to what he wants. In fact, he said take it all, he could get more.

There are many stories told to me about acts of sharing.

Mother talked about a Mexican whose first name was José. She called him "Spy-ola." He taught them how to take care of corn.

My oldest uncle Stern Two Bulls, who was born 18 days after Wounded Knee, started digging a well close to his house. It was about 8 feet wide and more than 5 feet deep.

José built a big fire that had a deep bed of coals in the hole. Then they brought several wagon loads of white corn, husks and all, and dumped them on top of the coals.

Then they poured several buckets of water, put tarps over, then shoveled dirt on top trapping all the heat and water.

The next morning they got the dirt and tarps off and had lots of steamed corn which they braided some, cut others, and put them on drying racks.

I never knew of corn being done like that.

That generation tried their best at taking care of themselves and their families.

Different families would buy the renderings of fat maybe from the packing plant. They called it "crackling," and used it to flavor gravy and soup and other foods.

Mother told me about one family that ate soup made from fat and fresh Russian thistle sprouts.

Inspired by our way of life, destroyed by the Government over more than a century, we have, for the most part, become entitlement people who are still struggling with many problems.

I often wonder how my peoples' life would be if the Government left us alone.

Chapter 4

Three Generations of Boarding School Experience

Some years ago, Alan Aker wrote an article concerning Governor Round's plan to teach Lakota Culture to our Students. He said it would accomplish nothing unless the story is told in its entirety, including teaching the truth about what the Government did to the Lakota people as well, and what they did to other Native tribes.

He mentioned teaching about the Government boarding schools that young Native children were forced to attend.

After reading Aker's article, I wanted to tell some personal boarding school experiences as well as other stories that were passed down to me.

I would like the reader to put themselves in the Lakota's place and honestly examine their feelings and think how their lives would be affected if they had some of those experiences.

These stories cover three generations starting with the 1800s to 1946 when my personal boarding school days ended. I can only express my own feelings and how I believe it affected me my whole life.

In the 1800s we Lakota people lived under a military rule which took away our rights. We were controlled by the Government and churches back east. The Lakota people, as well as other Native tribes, had no choice in what the Government plan was to educate their children.

My father's father, Oliver Swallow, was born in 1870. Grandpa Swallow was sent to a school in Philadelphia, Pennsylvania. It was a school created for civil war orphans. It was called Lincoln Institute.

The Government was trying an experiment to see if Indians could be educated.

He was sent in 1880 when he was ten years old. He didn't come home till he was sixteen years old.

Grandpa Swallow was a very positive man and for whatever reason he said very little about that time.

He did belong to a baseball team. He also got farmed out to a Dutch family who were farmers during that time.

Grandpa Swallow's mother was a Brule Lakota who left with Spotted Tail's band to Rosebud.

Grandpa Swallow spent six years growing up at the Lincoln Institute. He said when he first left for Lincoln Institute at a border town in Nebraska, they were all waiting for the train. When the train came charging down the tracks with a billowing stream of smoke and the whistle blowing, everyone scattered like prairie chickens having never seen a train before.

Grandpa and the others were loaded in a cattle car and left for Philadelphia.

My mother, Lizzie Two Bulls Swallow, was born in 1907 and lived on Red Shirt Table. My mother's generation was the first generation that went to boarding school. Her parents could not talk or understand English.

Mother said the first time they heard English her brother Pete made noise and slapped the palm of his hand on his mouth. She said that was how English sounded.

Mother talked about going to boarding school where they were forbidden to talk Lakota.

Mother went to B.I.A. boarding school in Pine Ridge for six years. Sixth grade was the highest grade taught, so mother and her siblings went to Rapid City Indian School til eighth grade.

I remember her talking about being punished for speaking Lakota, but she never said what type of punishment she received.

Although my Ant Edna Serry said when the full bloods got caught speaking Indian they were locked in a closet, where the only light getting in was from the bottom of the door.

Mother told me when her and her sister, Dora, and some of her brothers went to Rapid City Indian School their matron was ornery and mean spirited.

Mother's mother came to see her children. When she spoke to the matron, she had her daughter Dora translate. Grandma Two Bulls asked if she could take the girls downtown and buy them some things.

The matron scolded her and told her to leave the girls alone. They were there to learn.

Grandma Two Bulls was holding her baby who was about two years old. She handed the baby to Dora and grabbed the matron and shook her so hard the bun in her hair came loose and her eyes almost popped out.

That's what mother said, anyway. I guess she let them go downtown. Mother never said.

Mother talked about taking a home economics class and how she learned how to take care of meat, how to make pickles and a lot of other things she learned.

She also talked about the flu of 1918 in Pine Ridge where she saw wagons with caskets heading to the graveyard all day long. She remembered many children getting real sick. They drank lots of water and got lots of bed rest. She never said any children died.

I was born in 1939 and went to boarding school when I was six years old, my brother was nine, and sister was ten years old.

I remember when it was time for my parents to leave. I cried and begged to go home. I even promised to be good, which would have been a first for me.

My brother had to hold me while my parents left. My little sister, who was about two years old, gave me a halfhearted wave and left us alone.

My brother and I were standing in a semi-basement of the boy's dorm and I was sniffling. There were four boys looking at us, two of them about my age. One of them came up and asked me if I wanted to fight.

In a matter of three of four minutes I had hit both of the smaller boys. When one of the bigger boys came over, my brother fought him.

After that I got along with the little boys just fine. My brother was in many fights after that. I was proud of him because he could really fight. In later years, he told his oldest daughter that he liked to fight. I never cried for home after that.

We got into a routine of boarding school life. I don't remember of missing home or asking my brother questions about our parents.

Boarding school was my home.

I remember having two Indian matrons who took care of us little boys and made sure we showered. They folded our clothes and put them into our boxes. My box number was 48.

They also kept track of any money our parents left for us.

While I was in boarding school I had mumps, measles, chicken pox and I broke my arm. My mother wasn't there to hold me and comfort me during those hard times. I had to experience it on my own.

I came away from school with callous guarded feelings, tough and realistic.

I had a foul mouth which got me into a lot of trouble with my mother.

I remember us little boys had to wear coveralls and sometimes we would get a pair that had a flap in the back used for going bathroom. We were ashamed to wear them because we knew how to pull our pants down.

We would line up and marched to different activities.

I always liked Saturday nights because it was movie night. We watched updates on the war and a series that continued every week. I remember the series. A doctor Towbar was trying to take over the world. There was a scarlet horseman who wore a cape and mask and he was a good guy. He would hold up two fingers and the bad guys would chase him.

I used to walk around picking up orange peels and eating them. Maybe I lacked some sort of vitamin; all I know is that I like the taste.

North of the school in a low spot there was a potato field. When they would harvest potatoes they never managed to get every last one. We used to go down there and get potatoes and take them to the boiler room where there was hot cinders outside. We would dig a hole with a stick in the cinders and bury the potatoes. Sometimes we couldn't wait for them to cook so we would eat them half raw.

On Sundays we would put on one of the many little suits they had and we would head for church about three-fourths of a mile away. The Churches were Catholic, Presbyterian and Episcopal. I went to the Presbyterian Church.

Victor Swallow back row center, Presbyterian Church, Pine Ridge, South Dakota 1946.

I remember my mother would have terrible migraine headaches. She was in the hospital when we finally came home to stay. In later years, I asked her what they found out and she replied with "nerves."

I guess my boarding school days were uneventful compared to some of the Natives who first experienced boarding schools. NO mistreatment that I could remember.

Finally, when school was out, we were waiting to get on the bus for home with all of our papers and drawing to show our parents. I walked down to a nearby creek down the hill from the bus and threw my papers in the creek and watched them float away. My brother took his papers home to my parents and my mother asked where my papers were and told her I threw the into the creek.

Being home from school didn't take long to adjust to with different rules and getting along with others.

Once mother told me to do something and I cussed at her and took a swing at her and ran off. When she was mad she called me Victor instead of Vic. She said, "Victor get over here." I held up two fingers like the scarlet horseman and the chase was on. She eventually caught me and dragged me back to the house and washed my mouth with home-made lye soap. I never stopped cussing, but I never cussed in front of her or hit her again.

Decades later, I am a senior citizen now and looking back. I remember that little sister who waved at me and that nine year old boy who had to fight (I ended up enjoying fighting) and the young mother with the migraine headaches caused by nerves and the father who had no choice. All are gone.

I wish I could hold my mother again and cry with her over all the important years that were lost not only from her but from all of us.

Every day when the sunlight travels in from the East and a new day is coming, I think back to that time more than seventy years ago when the bond between a young mother and a little boy (who was only six years old) was broken. I am thankful that my children didn't have to experience their most important years of growing up away from home and family.

Chapter 5

The 1949 Blizzard

We are in the holiday season where families make a point to get together and spend time together and eat. This makes me think of old times when food wasn't always plentiful like during the 1949 Blizzard.

Looking back prior to the 1949 blizzard, we lived about six miles from Redshirt village which had a school. World War II was going on and the funding for bus service was stopped. Gas was being rationed.

People were struggling just to live.

My older sister Margaret was ten, my brother John Jr. was nine and I was six years old. We all went to Pine Ridge Boarding School for two years 1945-1947.

In 1947 a new school was started at the Red Shirt village it was an Adventist School.

Finally the war was over and people were starting to get ahead. My father rented Charlie Steel's house in Redshirt village for ten dollars a month and we lived there for two years only during the school year and went to school.

During the summer, we would move back on the table (Red Shirt Table) and plant a garden. We would harvest and mother canned the produce.

In 1948, father bought a new 1947 jeep, called a Willys Overland. It was a demonstrator and looked like an army jeep.

Father had a two-wheel trailer he used to get wood. He stock piled wood high at Charlie's house for the winter. He was always thinking ahead.

During the winter of 1949 it snowed for four days straight with high winds. We were still living at Charlie Steel's house. After it stopped snowing on the southside of the house the drift went all the way to the roof.

We were stranded.

I remember we had to shovel everywhere. To start, shovel a path to the outhouse and around the wood pile.

We had to melt snow for many days because the hydrant was under snow.

I often wondered how some of the families did on wood. I can remember two of my uncles Ed Two Bulls and Ed Fast Wolf had real big wood piles.

I know in the weeks after the storm a cargo plane flew real low and dropped food within walking distance for the community. We made it to where they dropped the food the whole community was digging through the snow.

We all were there picking through the food. Everyone was mindful of one another's family size and no one family got more than the others.

My parents had a cellar full of canned stuff and other garden produce on Redshirt Table but we were stranded in Redshirt village and no way to get to it.

The others in Redshirt village had gardens and cellars so I think they were able to get to their canned food.

I remember father put chains on the tires of the jeep and he could get around hitting the high spots. From the village down the (Cheyenne) river east there were a lot of dead cattle. Some of the cattle they didn't find till spring when all the snow melted.

The Cattlemen's Association lost a lot of cattle. I never did ask but father said they had 1300 head unit. It was never fully stocked. Father had 38 cows left and I don't remember how much he had prior to the blizzard.

The following year we stayed in the West end of the schoolhouse in one big room.

I remember looking through the Sears Roebuck catalog and I would wish for some combat boots that had two straps on the top, cleats on the front sole, and a pocket on the side for a pocket knife.

Father said if I gathered up the bones along the river he would take his trailer and haul them to Rapid City and sell them. He had to put a little money in and I got my boots.

I don't know what part the 1949 Blizzard played, but by 1954 almost all the cattle were sold off and life was never the same in Redshirt. Several families moved away and father got another loan and he bought more cattle and had a 175 head unit. He never fully stocked.

Now there are very few of us left of that community that lived through those hard times.

I remember my father bought a four-wheel trailer and was able to haul twelve foot logs. I imagine people prepared for the winer differently after the blizzard.

There are very few of us that lived through the 1949 blizzard that are still living ranged in age from infants to fourteen years of age.

Here are the ones that lived in Redshirt community that I could remember. My cousins starting with the oldest were Bob Two Bulls, Florence Ten Fingers, Francis Two Bulls, Delbert Yellow Horse, Elmarie Yellow Horse-Boyd and Julia Two Bulls-Garnier who was about 3 years old when it happened.

Also Evert Poor Thunder was my brother's age and his sister, Edith, was the same age as my sister Margret. Ethel was about my age who lived on Redshirt table. Silas Sound Sleeper also lived on the table.

I hope I haven't left anybody out. We were at least 5 years old and older when the blizzard took place. Doris Two Bulls was about 2 years old. I am not sure if she would remember anything from the blizzard but maybe she heard stories as she grew up.

There are so many stories connected to the 1949 Blizzard. This is my experience from a nine year old's perspective.

As I spent Thanksgiving with my family with plenty of food to go around, I can't help but think of the 1949 Blizzard when food was scarce.

I hope this story reminds you of how important family is and even when times are tough the most important thing is that everyone is together and doing ok.

I often wonder how many people who lived through the 1949 blizzard shared their experiences with anyone. I know I didn't until now.

We should all make a point to tell our loved ones, especially our young, some of the stories we lived through as we grew up. It will not only be entertaining but it will give them some history, their history.

Enjoy the Holiday Season with your loved ones.

Chapter 6

Early Christian Religions of Red Shirt Table

The last writing I wrote about something I've stayed away from since I have been writing which is politics. With Republicans no matter how bad the behavior of the leaders are, they say the bad one's are the "No good liberals."

Thinking about religion with the major Christian church which is the Catholic church who have moral and legal issues with crimes against children which has been going on for many decades with no change. Just business as usual but to them judgmental religious people who look at gays and transgenders within our communities as evil people and think they are bad ones. The truth is something we all should live and die by even when it hurts.

This writing will be about the religions that came to Red Shirt Table and funny things that happened, at least they were funny to me.

My mother who was born in 1907 said the first time she heard English was at the Episcopal church. Her brother Pete made fun of how they sounded by slapping his mouth with his hand and making noise. She said she thought it sounded like English to her.

There were two religions at Red Shirt the other was Catholic.

This next story is about a priest that came and stopped at Grandpa Two Bulls place. He said he met the devil himself on the way to Red Shirt.

The priest said the guy was a mixed blood. He said he told this guy he would share his lunch with him if he could Baptize him and he agreed. They sat together and ate. After they were done eating the Priest went to the back of the buggy to get things ready. He heard the horse galloping away. He thought that was awful.

Another story I want to share is at the Catholic church about mom's Grandmother's brother Silas Fills the Pipe.

Silas was mad at someone in the church and he wouldn't go in the church. When they came out of church he would ride by on his horse looking straight ahead purposely not looking at them then he would do a quick chopping wave. This really bothered the members.

A funny story is about my cousin Rueben and Larry Fast Wolf. They hated confession and would leave the house.

The priest caught them home one time and they went into the bedroom. The priest was standing with his back away from the door so they decided to sneak out with Rueben going first. Rueben went out then held the door on

Larry. Rueben said Larry was in the bedroom confessing up a storm and his mom was mad at him.

I teased Larry in later years, I suppose you said, "I ate meat at Aunt Lizzie's last Friday and also farted in Rueben's face." He said he didn't remember what he said.

The other church that was at Red Shirt was the Seventh Day Adventist. They worshiped on Saturday and went with Jewish laws on clean and unclean meats and also had a school that went to the 10th grade that was the church I attended. Five of mom's siblings were members. (They weren't real strict members.)

Victor Swallow (front row bibs), brother John Swallow (far left, middle row with plaid jacket and winter cap), sister Margret Swallow (far right back row with head scarf and full face view), Jimmy Fast Wolf (is the tallest far back row), Edith Poor Thunder (near center second row from back with head scarf full face view with eye glasses), the rest are all Victor Swallows first cousins from the Two Bull family.

The minister told my mom he went to visit my Uncle Jake. Uncle Jake must have felt guilty about something. The minister said, "Brother Jake was under the bed hiding but his feet were sticking out."

The members slowly left the church. My sister Margret Dyer was the last devout Adventist when her husband passed away. He was cremated.

Months later she came to my house and asked me how her husband was going to get out of the urn. I told her if you can believe you will pop out of the ground and be made whole again, you should be able to believe he'll get out of the urn. Margret then said, "That's right."

I believe modern day man is frail and insecure and we need a crutch to deal with everyday life. Some peoples crutch can be booze, drugs, psychiatrist, guns while others look to religion. What I write are real stories and I hope some people find them interesting.

Some years back a friend of mine and I were going to a funeral at the Catholic church. As we topped the hill south of Red Shirt village he asked me what I believed. I pointed to Blind Man's Table to a stand of cedar trees and said there are probably some deer, coyotes or rabbits that are there and maybe a hawk or eagle flying over head. Whatever they believed is what I believe. If you believe in a creation, respect others who believe otherwise.

We all have the same beginning, grow to maturity, reproduce, then begin to grow older and eventually die.

Many of us humans contribute to our own demise.

Chapter 7

Red Shirt Table Teenage Boys Willing to Work Hard for Local Ranchers

I am going to write about experiences I had as a young man working with mostly my cousins. I call ourselves the Red Shirt Table boys which consisted of my brother Johnny Swallow, Rueben Fast Wolf, Orville Two Bulls, Silas Sound Sleeper, and Lawrence Two Bulls.

Back then the job opportunities were very few. Some of us worked for local ranchers in 1955. My brother Johnny and I went to work irrigating for a guy over in Oral (SD) for $3 a day and room and board. That didn't work out. He wanted us to wait till he harvested his corn and sold it and we weren't going to do that. We ended up hitching hiking home.

Our father had cattle so we always had something to do. Reuben Fast Wolf, our cousin, went to work for a guy named Tad Clark. I don't know how long but he earned from Tad a nice red 1951 Ford, 2 door that ran real good.

My brother, Peter, and Francis Two Bulls went to Rapid City and worked roofing hangers out to Ellsworth Air

Force (base). I was stacking hay for a rancher whose name was Wes Harrison.[a]

All of us Red Shirt boys were willing to work.

When a big company out of Chicago Norris Grainery or Stock Yard, I'm sure of the Norris name....

They brought up ranchers throughout the upper midwest. The ranches that I remember are the Hart Stienger Ranch, Miller Ranch, and Battle Creek ranch.

The Western Cattle Company hired many people from all over the state. Many were from Red Shirt, Hermosa and surrounding communities. It was the first job for many of the boys from Red Shirt. They had a fencing crew, hay crew and other crews. They paid 8 1/2 dollars a day to run tractors and 15 dollars a day to stack hay which was what my bother and I did.[b]

The man in charge of the haying crew was a little guy named Ray Stable Felts who was from the Hermosa area. All the equipment was brand new.

I only worked there one summer so the following stories are my brother's stories he told me. Ray knew how to get along with the Red Shirt Table boys and they liked to joke around and play pranks on each other.

---

[a] Ellsworth Air Force Base, located ten miles east of Rapid City, began as a Rapid City Army Air Base in 1941. In 1942 it became a training base for the Army Air Force B-17 Flying Fortress. From 1948-1958 Ellsworth operated as the 28th Bombardment Wing flying B-29 Superfortress bombers as a permanent base for the U.S. Air Force.

[b] Western Cattle Company was a division of Norris Grain Company that operated and managed between an estimated 350,000-500,000 acres of mostly grazing land on various ranches in South Dakota.

One time Orville Two Bulls tied a bull snake to the steering wheel of the farmhand tractor. I can imagine what it looked like when Ray found the snake.

Another time was when Ray and Orville were wrestling. They were about the same size with no one getting the best of the other. Ray teased Orville saying all the boys at Red Shirt were scared to wrestle him.

Silas Sound Sleeper's brother, Pat, stopped by to talk to Silas. Ray told Orville he was going over and asked Pat if he wanted to wrestle. Pat talked broken English and talked through his nose. He was about the same size as Ray who walked over to Pat who was a few years younger.

Ray said to Pat, "You want to wrestle?" Pat said, "No." Ray said, "Come on Pat lets wrestle!" Pat again said no! Ray threw his hands up and went back to Orville and said, "See I told you," referring to the Red Shirt Table boys not wanting to wrestle. So they went back to work.

Pat goes on to Hermosa and buys a 1/2 gallon of wine and nurses on it for several hours. Pat now feeling in a wrestling mood headed for the hay fields. He gets there and hollers at Ray, "Come on Ray lets wrestle!" Ray ignored him and kept driving his farm equipment. Everyone had a good laugh at Ray's expense.

The Western Cattle Company employed many people over the years with many good memories. The people I know that worked for the cattle company and are still alive are; Silas Sound Sleeper, Marvin Cuny, Francis Thompson, Wayne Morgan and myself.

Looking back, when I was a teenager on the verge of adulthood with no major responsibilities I think about all of us Red Shirt Table boys who took advantage of opportunities to earn some money. We were all willing to work hard!

Chapter 8

Red Shirt Table Story

Most of the stories I write about way back when are told to me by my mother Lizzie Two Bulls-Swallow. When I re-tell these stories told to me I always acknowledge the person who told me.

My mother told me how Red Shirt Table was settled which was told to her by her father Fred Two Bulls (my grandpa). My mother said that Grandpa Two Bulls knew an Indian Agent and he told him the Cheyenne River area what is now known as Red Shirt Table would be allotted soon. The Indian Agent told my Grandpa Two Bulls he should go up there and pick a spot he liked and build a house and make improvements and that land would be his.

Somewhere around the year 1900, different families started moving to the Cheyenne River area most were from Manderson.

In 1907 my mother was born and in 1909 is when the Indian Agent came through to allotted the land. He allotted the Head of the household 640 acres, wife 320 acres, and each child 160 acres.

When my Grandpa Two Bulls got his land allotted he told the Indian Agent I also got a baby in the tent. The

Agent asked to see the baby so my Grandpa Two Bulls got the baby from the tent, which was my mother Lizzie Two Bulls and showed the Indian Agent. At the time my Grandpa had eight children who got land allotted and three more children were born after.

I was always interested in history, especially about the area and people where I grew up. I found a book of a diary of a Pine Ridge Government official at the School of Mines and he wrote that Chief Red Dog took his people and went to the Cheyenne River area. He also wrote that Red Dog was non progressive and lived to an old age.

Mother talked about old man Red Dog who lived below in Cedar Creek Canyon between Red Shirt Table and Blind Man's Table. When she was a young girl, she remembered hearing Red Dog beating his drum and singing at daybreak and at dusk. She said it sounded lonesome. I don't know what happened to Red Dog, she never told me.

I am grateful that my Grandpa Fred Two Bulls had the foresight to go to a new area and start a new beginning for his children's future where they could look to the East and see the Badlands and look the West and see the Black Hills. To this day the original allotments are still being utilized by the Two Bulls descendants.

Chapter 9

The Red Shirt Table Experiment

I have been retired for 15 years and had lots of time to reflect on my life.

I know of my parents and grandparents from 1870 to the present time. I have done my own research of reading books of the history of Lakota people and their dealings with the U.S. Government. I have been reasoning things out and forming opinions from my gathered information and knowledge and here is a story that shows a little about the effect of what the government did to us Lakotas.

In the late 1930s, I suppose in hopes to try to assimilate us Lakotas the Government helped with building an irrigation system to help water their gardens, building of a local school, adding a turkey farm, and loaned ten men, including my dad who lived on Red Shirt Table, a replacement plan of cattle.

This plan was for each of the ten individuals to start with cattle and in later years they were to give back the Government that same amount.

During the summer they harvested their produce and picked wild berries and canned it for the winter. They dug wild turnip and peeled them and braided them to dry to cook in soup for the winter. They butchered a cow and dried the meat. My father trapped coyotes and rabbits to and sold their fur. Their cellars were full of canned goods, garden produce and dried meat that was used to get us through the winter.

During the fall they had a Fair with a B.I.A. employee judging the produce and the canned goods and giving out ribbons.

One year they shipped their calves to Sioux City. My father said they topped the market and were doing pretty good. The B.I.A. regulated their herds in 1949.

We had a terrible blizzard the lasted for days. The Cattlemen's Association lost many of their cattle. I don't know the year all the loans the families took out with the Government got paid back. I don't remember if it was before or after the 1949 Blizzard. What I do know is that my dad trailed his cattle to Blacktail south of the casino.

Why he did that, he never said, he had about 40 head and he trucked them back, I don't know when.

The B.I.A. turned the management of cattle to the individuals and by 1954 the others sold their cattle. My father sold his cattle in 1961 a year after my brother and I went in the service.

All ten of these men were born from 1891 to 1919 and were the first generation to go to school in large numbers at least to the sixth grade. They all talked good English and did business in Rapid City but in the end went back to the traditional way as it was before they had cattle.

Looking back after several decades of time to witness and ponder why this happened is all predictable.

The Government that controls every aspects of your life like where you live, the food you received down to the cattle that was given was all regulated. These were all aspects foreign to them and they learned how to adjust and try to adapt to this new way of providing for their families.

Once the regulation was lifted and the responsibility was given to each family to do as they pleased. They chose to sell all their cattle and ended up back where they started.

Several years back in Rapid City there was a statue on the corner of 6th street and Main street by Prairie Edge of a Lakota Warrior in chains. That statue symbolizes what happened to us Lakota people.

I want the World to know of what happened to us Lakotas and why we are the way we are and how we got here.

I wish that statue was still there along with the facts that tell our story. Us Lakotas dwell on pettiness when we should be trying to tell the story of the Government dealings with us Lakotas in our school systems because there are people out there that have empathy and good hearts and from that they would understand that's why we are the way we are.

This is my own opinion of this matter and what I was told from my parents and nothing more.

Chapter 10

The Summer Cattle Drive of 1949

Of the many stories I have written about, this next story is one of my most memorable experiences with my family. This is a story of a cattle drive that took place in 1949.

My father John Swallow, mother Lizzy Two Bulls-Swallow, and my three siblings ranged from 6 to 14 years old. I was 10 years old.

I believe it was 38 cows with some calves and it was approximately 45 miles total of our journey traveled. The journey started at Red Shirt Table to south of the casino in a community called Black Tail where my father was raised. I don't know the circumstances why he move his cattle that year, I can only guess.

My father had belonged to a Cattlemen Association that had their loans paid up and were starting to sell their cattle. In his writing he mentioned people had sold some cattle that weren't branded.

My father was a loner and didn't like belonging to any organization that he didn't have a say or any control of his part in the association.

On the first day of the cattle drive I remember we got a late start from Redshirt and traveled ten or twelve miles. I took my turn herding cattle. Dad had a jeep and it was pulling a hay rack with a tent and all our belonging and provisions in it for the journey.

We would spend the summer at Grandpa Oliver Swallow's place.

The first night we set up the tent and dad started a fire. Mom made dried meat soup with fat, onions, potatoes and rice. I loved that soup even to this day.

The next morning she cooked oatmeal and we ate the rest of that soup for breakfast. In later days she fried potatoes and made skillet bread.

I remember a year earlier we were in that area and I shot my brother with a wham-o sling shot I bought myself. My dad made me throw it off to the side of the road after which my brother made faces at me. I wished I didn't shoot him. At least I didn't get a spanking.

On the second day I remembered where my dad made me throw out my wham-o sling shot. I rode over to the place where I threw it out and the clutch to my wham-o was dried and split and the rubber had rotted and the leather dried up.

We finally made it to White River and that night we camped near the old No Water homestead.

My mother always cooked something good and I loved to eat. Sometime when dad rode horseback my older sister drove the jeep. It took us four days to get there.

Grandpa Swallow looked like a white man but would visit my mother in Lakota. My mother's first language was Lakota. He still rode horseback at 79 years old. Then later my dad trucked this cattle back, I don't know when.

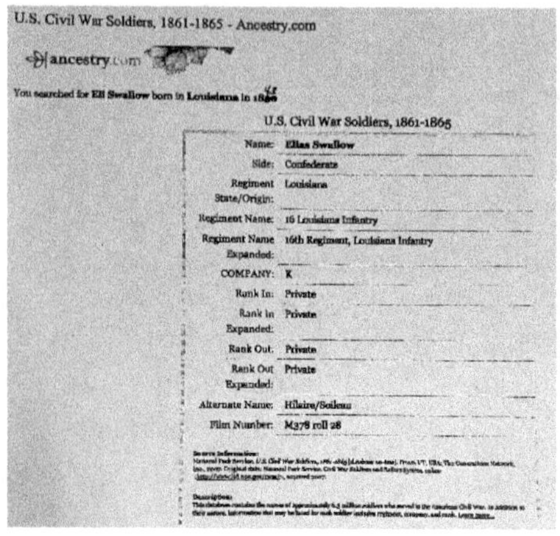
U.S. Civil War Soldiers, 1861-1865 - Ancestry.com

ancestry.com

You searched for Eli Swallow born in Louisiana in 18[illegible]

U.S. Civil War Soldiers, 1861-1865

Name:	Elias Swallow
Side:	Confederate
Regiment State/Origin:	Louisiana
Regiment Name:	16 Louisiana Infantry
Regiment Name Expanded:	16th Regiment, Louisiana Infantry
COMPANY:	K
Rank In:	Private
Rank In Expanded:	Private
Rank Out:	Private
Rank Out Expanded:	Private
Alternate Name:	Hilaire/Soileau
Film Number:	M378 roll 28

Source Information: [illegible]

Description: [illegible]

Grandpa had a big two story house with four bedrooms. Two bedrooms on both floors. He was born at the Wetstone Agency in 1870 to Eli Swallow and Lizzie Iyotte. Lizzie was part of the Spotted Tail's band.

My grandpa had three brothers and one sister. He lived alone and had one daughter that lived a little over a mile away from him. There are many stories to be told about grandpa Swallow.

He would saw wood for immediate use and also he stocked piled it for the long winter. I would sit on a log while he would saw and listen to him tell stories.

One story he told me that he was there digging a well and so far down there was a big rock. When they moved it to one side a big bull frog jumped out and they chased it on a race horse. They never did catch it.

I remember another story he told me his hired hand saw a big snake halfway to Red Shirt. It had a cows head, dad told me that grandpa's hired hand was full of it. My dad said when the hired hand told these stories to his mother I guess she believed some of them.

During that summer my brother and I had fun roaming around our Grandpa's land of 640 acres that had a creek on it. One day we ran into a skunk and my brother Johnny said he would tease it and I was to go around and grab it by the tail. My brother said he wouldn't pee on me.

Later that day my mother wouldn't let me into the house. That's when I should have used my sling shot.

Later that summer I got another one. The crutch was from a choke cherry tree and the rubber was from a cut inner tube and leather from an old shoe.

We spent the whole summer at my grandpa's place and I got to know him better. We had a good summer that time.

As grandpa got older he moved in with his daughter. She had chickens, ducks, geese and he took care of them.

Grandpa was up and taking care of chores and turned in to bed for the evening and never woke up. He lived to be 87 and my dad 93.

I know many people don't get to experience moments like these. This was unique for me and I am grateful for my parents for giving me these moments.

This cattle drive is a part of my life's history which I'm proud of. I encourage the readers to spend more time with their families. When I ask my kids what are some of the most memorial experiences they remember as a kid they always say times we spent together as a family.

Chapter 11

A Tribute to a Lakota Woman with Strong Lakota Values

As Lakotas most of us never get the chance to share our experiences of reservation life beginning with our grandparents and their generation, our parents and then our own personal experiences, and also people from other reservations.

Us Lakota people do well in honoring our dead, honoring our people who serve or served in the military, also those that are educated, and have done well in life.

There are many living that should be acknowledged. This is my tribute to a special Lakota woman from Cheyenne River who lived her life with Lakota values and her love of family, empathy and respect for others, and above all a lady with a good heart. Unfortunately she has passed away decades ago and this is her story.

Her name is Loretta Fern Laplante and she was born in the early 1900s and lived to the age of early 80s. Most people called her by her middle name Fern. I met her in 1971, she was my wife's aunt. I have respect and good feelings towards her and her family.

Fern lived in the small community of White Horse which is on the Cheyenne River Reservation. She was the cook for the White Horse School for many years. Fern was well known in the Timber Lake (SD) area and respected by natives and whites alike. She raised many children over the years. Fern raised her own daughter along with her husband's three younger children.

When her sister passed away, she took her two boys and adopted them and raised them. She took the youngest right away and then the older one later.

Fern also raised a younger sister from her father's second marriage from when she was ten years old.

Fern also raised a brother's daughter who was living with her when she passed away.

Fern had compassion for people and took upon herself to care for the elderly.

Mr. and Mrs. Warrior who was born in the late 1800s and George Phillips and also a Bull Marshall.

Much of this information I got from one of Fern's sister's sons who said she raised, Lanny Laplante.

When I think of all the kids over the years that Fern raised and made a difference in their lives to keep them with family, I can only smile!

When Fern knew my wife and family were coming to visit, she would make me a pot of dried meat soup. She knew I liked that! She made me feel welcome in her home. As we stayed in her house for several days while we visited my wife's relatives in White Horse.

Many people would call or stop in to visit and drink coffee. There is no doubt Fern touched many lives and when people think of her, their memories are always good!

There are others among us that have qualities like Fern and as humble as they are never know how much they truly impact the world with their kind acts.

A few years ago, we honored Fern's longer sister Vallie Laplante and I remember how touched she was that so many people gathered to hold a special dinner to appreciate her. Vallie was overwhelmed with gratitude and emotion that she couldn't even address all the friends and relatives.

Honoring dinners like that need to take place for special people in our lives before it is too late. Don't wait to honor someone when they are gone to remember their good deeds. Have a special day just for them to let them know they are appreciated and loved.

Life is short and waiting could end up being to late.

Fern was a strong pillar of the White Horse community, not just for her relatives but for the whole community.

I will leave with a conversation I had with my Aunt Dolores Two Bulls. I told her that the Cheyenne River people treat me better than my own people and she replied, "That's because they don't know you like we know you. You're a pest," she said with a smile on her face.

Chapter 12

A Trip to Crow Agency in 1966

I will write this story just the way it happened. I was 27 years old and out visiting relatives at Red Shirt when one of my uncles came to me he was half shot.

My uncle asked me if he could hire me to take my aunt and a cousin who was about twelve years old to Montana to see his daughter who was married to a Crow Indian. I didn't want to put up with him so I said no!

Then my aunt who was a kind and humble woman came and asked me and I couldn't say no to her. We left for Montana.

All the way up to Montana my uncle tried to get me to stop at every liquor store. Finally in Ashland, Montana he said my aunt and cousin wanted some pop so I stopped at a grocery store. He got out walked across the street to a liquor store and came out with a jug. He nipped the rest of the way.

We got to a home of a man whose name was Hugh Plenty Hoops who was married to Yellow Tail's daughter. Yellow tail is a well know Crow Indian quite successful.

It was in the late afternoon Hugh's wife was dressed like my grandmother with a long dress with moccasins with leggings. She was very kind and caring person.

My uncle was feeling his oats teasing me saying were there any females around that would have me. He didn't care what they looked like just anybody would do since I was single.

After Hugh's wife fed us, Hugh had been heating some rocks for his sweat lodge he had close to a mountain stream. He asked us to sweat with him.

In the sweat lodge he said he was going to first pray for us and our families then he would pray for his country and lastly he would pray for his family. This wasn't a fad or something recent—it was their way of life from the old days of their kindness and generosity ways.

I will always remember Hugh running my uncle and myself out of the sweat lodge. We jumped into the cold mountain stream which was chest high and uncle was sober as a judge after that.

Later they took us in a 4-wheel drive pickup pulling a trailer into the mountains. We stayed overnight in an old Civilian Conservation Corp (C.C.C.) cabin. We shot three deer and Hugh's wife roasted a front quarter with the ribs, fried some potatoes and made squaw bread with coffee all over an open fire.

It was a time I will always remember. Unfortunately, they are all gone now even my cousin the twelve year old.

My uncle and his friend Hugh and his wife were all second generation out of the wild. I believe that second generation of natives all had good hearts!

Chapter 13

Bird All Over

George Catlin, who was a Naturalist traveled West in the 1830s, was known as an American painter, author and traveler who focused his work on Native Americans and studied 18 tribes. I read one of his writings about his observations of Native Americans.

Catlin paid tribute to Native Americans in a writing in part it says, "I love a people who made me welcome to the best that they had, who are honest without laws, who worship God without a Bible, who have no Religious animosities and how I love a people who don't live for the love of money." These are the kind of people we Natives come from.

Stories I write are stories told to me by my mother and father as to them from relatives who lived from the 1840's to the 1940's.

I will start with stories about hardships our people endured when the way of life ended and how they survived. Still proud. We are Lakota. Human interest stories I focus on trying to be positive and interesting in a negative world.

The following story is about my mother's grandmother her name was Bird All Over. She was born in the late 1840s. She had two brothers, Silas Fills the Pipe and Elias Kills One Hundred. Bird All Over was married to a half breed named Two Buffalo Bulls or Two Bulls or sometimes called him Two Buffaloes they had six children together four boys and two girls.

Bird All Over married a second time to a man named Brave Heart. Mother never mentioned her or her husbands having first names.

In later years, when my mother's family went to bed her grandmother Bird All Over would be talking about when they roamed free. She was born somewhere along Rapid Creek (draining from the Black Hills of South Dakota).

Mother would stay up trying to hear her stories but would be so tired she would go to sleep for a little while then wake up. When she would wake up, my mother said my grandmother would still be talking.

Mother said she wished she had stayed awake and heard all of her stories.

Several stories she remembered was one she told my wife. She said grandmother Bird All Over said when they were issuing rations they got sacks of flour among the rations and didn't know what it was used for. So they dumped out the flour and made dresses out of the sacks.

Some Lakota lady who married a white man asked for the flour and everybody gave her the flour. Not once did they bother to ask her what she did with the flour. Later someone finally asked what the lady used the flour for and she taught them how to make bread with it.

She said in later years they got hungry for fresh meat so they killed a bunch of swallow birds and ate them and got constipated. Mother called it "Bound up."

Mother told me about her brothers Stern and Edward working the hills taking her and her grandmother Bird All Over to help baby sit. They camped in the hills so they would be close to work.

Mother and her grandmother Bird All Over would stay back at camp with the kids. All day long big dump trucks would pass by making a lot of dust up in the air. This made grandmother Bird All Over mad so she would be waiting with her fist clenched up facing her fist towards the on coming dump trucks. When the trucks would pass by she straightens her fingers out.

Older Lakotas know this to be a gesture of disgust.

Mother said as each truck approached their camp that her grandmother Bird All Over would have her fist clenched waiting for the truck to go by.

Mother said in her grandmother's waning years, having lost her sense of reality, she wandered among the sage brush south of Fred Two Bulls home on Red Shirt Table talking to herself.

Mom never did say what happened to her and how she died. Grandmother Bird All Over saw many changes in her life including loss of freedom being the greatest change.

Chapter 14

Depression Area 1

These two stories are about life in the late 1920s to early 1930s. Both stories are during the depression when money was scarce, people bartered for their necessities, and hard work was a part of everyday life.

My mother told me that some people were from Pine Ridge. Others were from Red Shirt Table and they would go to Deadwood's Annual Celebration where they would be paid for their performance. The agreement of payment for their services was money and a fat cow.

My mom said after they had got settled in, several riders came driving down the road with a bony old milk cow. She said the spokesman representing them was name Jake White Cow Killer. He told them, "You promised us a fat beef, so take that boney cow away and bring us what you promised or all of us will go home."

So they took the old milk cow away and brought a fat cow to replace it.

Hearing this story my mother told me makes me think about how deceit and wrong-doing has been going on for over 500 years and will continue in the future.

I would hope people would live by the "Golden Rule" like I was taught to treat others the way you want to be treated. But I am a Realist and that don't seem realistic, not in today's world. It seems like some people are willing to do other people wrong just to get ahead.

This next story is about potato picking and about a man with a good heart.

People from Red Shirt had gone to Scotts Bluff-Gering area in Nebraska to harvest produce. They would get paid and also get some produce to take home with them.

Mother said it was during the (1930s) Depression and the farmer said he was taking a load of potatoes to town and he would be back to pay them.

When he came back mother said he had tears in his eyes and he told them he didn't get very much money. He said he would give them half of the money he got because his wife needed some things but they could have all the potatoes and beans they wanted.

They took what they could carry and went back to Red Shirt.

Mom said her cousin Amos Iron Plume was there and had $20, she didn't know where they got it. They hired a truck and went back to Nebraska and got 800 pounds of potatoes and 200 pounds of beans. They had something to eat all winter.

Stories like these need to be told on how life was after reservations were created and the hardships they endured.

Most of the Indians were humble and happy and didn't dwell on their mistreatment and the lies the Federal Government told them. It was a Government with no conscience, guilt or shame. This is coming from a realist with no bitterness, just based on fact who did OK in life.

Victor's wife, Melidie's parents, Nelson and Elverna Miner, lived near Timber Lake, South Dakota on the Cheyenne River Reservation. Photo taken some time in the 1940s.

Chapter 15

Halloween Memories with Family

This time of year I look outside and see the leaves on the trees changing color and briskness of the air starts to set in. I think about the past and all the memories I have and the experiences I had over the years and the best memories I have are the moments with family.

I think about Halloween coming up and I don't have any stories that my mother told me or any stories about my own childhood Halloween stories. I only have stories that took place after I married and had kids.

I remember it was the year when people were putting razor blades and poison in the kids candy. It was big. It made the news. So my wife Melidie Swallow and her Sister-in-Law, Shirley Miner, decided to have a Halloween party instead of letting the kids go trick-or-treating.

They went shopping and planned out games for the kids to play and made candy bags for them. All the kids got to invite a friend and they all dressed up in costumes.

I know my wife wanted me to dress up as well. My wife Melidie went as Aunt Jemima and I went as an old man.

I think back on that moment over thirty--five years ago and today the wife and I after years of aging we would just go as ourselves and we would look like we dressed up.

I could go a bit further and rat up my thinning white hair so it stands straight up and take out my false teeth and really scare the trick-or-treaters that knock on our door.

The games they played for entertainment were ballon shaving, bobbing for apples, drop a bean into a glass pop bottle, and the dress up relay.

The relay was the best because we made two teams according to gender. The girls had to dress up like men with suit and tie and the boys had to dress up like women with a bra and high heels.

They had to run down and quickly put on the clothes run across the room take off the cloths then the next person in line does the same thing. It was really funny watching the boys put on bras and run in high heels.

A few years ago all my kids were at the house and that Halloween party came up in conversation. I didn't realize all my kids said that that year we did the Halloween party was a good childhood memory for them. It was good for me to know that all our kids and their friends had a safe good time that year!

A few years ago my daughter Vikki wanted to host a Halloween party at our house. We invited our granddaughter and her three boys and our other granddaughter who is a teenager now and her friend. The rest of us were adults and we all dressed up.

My niece, Val Spencer-Washington, showed up as a cat. Her mother is my cousin, Freida Two-Bulls-Spencer, who is gone now.

We did a potluck and all the desserts consisted of Oreo cookie witches hats, chocolate pretzel spiders and rice crispy treat Frankenstein's. After we ate, we played three Halloween games—eyeball blowout, spider throw down, and traveling ghost teeth.

It was nice to see all of my great grandchildren to have such fun! All of us adults had fun too! Time with family always is a good time. We just laugh and get silly when we are together.

I encourage everyone to go back to the old Lakota values where family is one of the most important things. A person doesn't have to have a lot of money to make their kids feel special—just spend time with them and ask them about their lives.

I encourage any of you to make a point to get together with your family to continue to create those moments that your kids, grand kids and great grandkids will always remember for the rest of their lives.

Chapter 16

The 4th of July Celebrations Experienced Through Three Generations

As I get older I look forward to attending celebrations with good food and visiting with friends and family.

Recently I celebrated 4th of July with my family barbecuing and visiting. This reminds me of past celebrations I experienced as a child. I'm going to write about the 4th of July celebrations that I remember.

For my first celebration, I believe I was four years old and it was during World War II. Gas was being rationed so dad took a team and wagon from Red Shirt to Oglala.

The 4th of July celebrations were a big deal among the Lakota people. I was never told that the celebration was because of Independence Day. I don't think anyone knew why they were celebrating. I think it was an excuse to get together camp, cook out and enjoy one another's company.

What little I remember I was sleeping in the wagon and we hit a big bump. I sat up and looked around. We were close to Wolf Mount Hill which is halfway to Oglala.

When we got to dad's uncle George Gillispie's place the sun was going down. I remember the other kids there were Edna May and Kitty Belle.

The next morning we went to the celebration which was over the hill southeast of Lone Man. The one thing I remember is sleeping in the wagon and hearing singing and the drums beating.

The second 4th of July I remember I was eight years old and it was south of Number 6 Day School. There were many tents and a few tepees. It's hard to guess how many people were there but there were lots of tents.

There was a rodeo area, a shade and a fenced area for a white dance. There were many beautiful horses prancing around. At the rodeo was a sorrel bucking horse they called Starlite.

Later when we got home from the celebration behind the chicken coop there was a rodeo going on. My brother and I would play with our homemade bone horses replaying Starlite's performance with lots of farting noises.

My father was born in 1910 and was raised along Black Tail Creek south of the (Prairie Wind Hotel and) Casino. He told me when he was a boy he would go to Oglala for the 4th of July celebration.

During the celebrations there was Indian dancing. Sometimes it lasted for three days. He had many relatives along White River who were decedents of David Talton Gillispie and Sara Long Jaw Gillispie.

Sara was full blooded Cheyenne who was married to a white man from Missouri. They had eight children who all lived in the Oglala area.

Dad mentioned that one time at the camp there was an old man walking. He knelt down and relieved himself and continued walking. Nobody paid attention they just went about their business.

Dad said after three days when the celebration ended the people wanted to go another day. Since they were all still camped they had someone ask the Superintendent if they can celebrate another day.

The Superintendent said, "No they have already been celebrating for three days. That's enough they need to pack up and go home." Dad said it was quite a sight to see all the team and wagons, lots of horses and dust.

In 1979 my brother Johnny's family and my family went to Wakpamhi's 4th celebration. It was well organized. There was plenty to do with a softball tournament, pow wow and a cross country six mile run.

I remember we watched dancing in the morning and it was mostly kids. One chubby girl about twelve years old danced so hard she had to stop and pull up her under clothes. My brother said she danced right out of her pants.

Together our kids ranged in age from one year to sixteen years old.

Denby Dam was close by so Johnny and I took the boys fishing. It was the best celebration gathering I've been to. I never saw one drunk.

A few years later Johnny's family and mine celebrated 4th of July a little more patriotic. We bought fireworks and went camping for the weekend along the edge of the Badlands on Red Shirt. My kids were between the ages of eight and thirteen.

I remember for supper we were cooking hot dogs in a cast iron skillet over an open fire. Clouds came in and it started to rain. We all took cover in the tents. It down poured for about 15 minutes. When we came out the fire was out and all the hot dogs were floating.

I asked my daughter Vikki what she remembers about that celebration and she said, "It was one of the best camping trips we had and I remember the hot dogs floating in the water after the rainstorm."

Later our kids had fun lighting off fireworks while us adults visited.

My brother has been gone for twelve years. Our kids are now in their 40's and 50's. These were a few of many of the good memories I had with my brother and his family.

Looking back at my childhood and thinking about all the plans my parents made and got the provisions ready for the celebration. I am grateful for the experiences they gave me. As a parent I found out how important it is to make plans to get together and make good memories with your own family.

Chapter 17

Shared Traits of Humans and Dogs

Over the years I took notice of animals behavior mostly dogs. I noticed similarities between dogs and humans.

The first story I am going to tell is about two dogs we had. They were outside dogs and shared a doghouse.

One dog was part terrier named Little Foot. He was black. The other was a small white poodle named Dante.

Little Foot was older by a few years. He was playful while Dante was crabby and would growl at Little Foot.

They got a long fairly well until it was time to eat. I would put one bowl right in the back of the house and the other bowl out of sight on the other side of the house.

Little Foot would guard both bowls preventing Dante from eating from either bowl. I had to be the regulator and I make sure Dante would get his fair share of food.

In later years as Little Foot got older he became partly blind. He would follow Dante all over the back yard. I believe Dante knew Little Foot couldn't see well and purposely walked slow so he could follow him.

The second story I had pulled a trailer over to Torrington, Wyoming where I was working on a college. One morning after breakfast I looked outside, there was a medium size black dog walking by. I called it over and gave him my leftovers. After that for three days he was waiting outside for more leftovers which I gave him. After the fourth day he was scratching at my door.

The third story happened shortly after we bought our house in 1973. I was out in the back yard and I saw a big police dog trotting up the alley. There was a little dog running beside it yipping and barking. The big dog had his head up not paying any attention to the one making all the noise, purposely ignoring his loud barking.

Over the years dogs have been a part of our lives as humans. We welcome them into our families and call them our best friends. They are very loyal and cheer us up when we are down. They guard our house and make us feel safe. Dogs will never abuse their young or abandon them.

They can be taught to do many things to help to improve our lives. We can look at the human race and find greedy selfish bullies that aren't willing to share like Little Foot.

We also have humans that make their living on getting handouts like the stray dog in Torrington.

There are also humans like Dante who get bullied over and over but when given an opportunity to help the bully, Dante didn't hold any grudges and helped Little Foot.

Like the police dog, there are humans who choose to ignore others and go about their business.

I think about what characteristics of a dog I display. I guess it depends on who you ask, my wife, my kids or people I have worked with, it all will vary I suppose. I just hope to treat people as I want to be treated.

Thinking about all of the dogs my family had over the years, I watched them grow up along with my kids, grandkids and great grandkids.

The one thing that reminds me how awesome dogs are is that they are always happy to see you. For example if you get mad at your dog for digging in the trash and making a mess and you send them outside, later when you invite them back in they are happy to see you.

Dogs look at us in a positive light and with love in their eyes as though we are amazing.

I heard a saying a number of years ago and I believe us humans should try to live by this saying, "Everyday I strive to be the person my dog thinks I am."

Chapter 18

Stories about the Mysterious and Unexplainable

I have always been a person who reads the newspaper and watch local and worldly news and it is hard to stay positive when you hear all the negative sides of the world. Our social media is more than willing to bring out the bad in any story because that is what sells and people like talking about all the drama.

My daughter Vikki always talks about having a newspaper that only highlights the good parts of the world because that is the side that is worth reading about.

Everyone makes bad choices. Why focus on those when most people have good aspects of who they are.

Looking back at our United States history and all the great measures people made through blood, sweat and tears to make our country a place of freedom. Great lengths people made so we can express ourselves freely.

Unfortunately now because of leadership examples us Americans live in a world where hate is become the normal.

Now days there are several reasons a person can hate another person. For example you can be hated for the color of your skin or for your beliefs or your economic status. People can dislike you for your political party or whether you are straight or otherwise. It is tolerated and made minimal.

Our world is struggling to right itself but we need to grab what is good and make that our priority.

What makes me feel good is reminiscing about the past when for the most part we didn't out right hate each other.

I will write about the mysterious things that happen in the animal world.

Things that people have seen all unexplainable can't seem to find logical ways to understand. I'm sure some readers have had experiences of this nature.

First I will write about my own experience which took place about fifteen years ago when my father passed away. The funeral service was held in Red Shirt gymnasium and a bird came into the gym and flew around. After the service was over they took my father out of the gym and the bird flew out the door.

Weeks later at that time I was working on skirting a trailer house on Red Shirt Table. I was wearing a baseball cap and I was sitting out in the shade. A bird came and sat on my head then hopped on the bill of my cap.

It was probably less than 10 seconds it flew and landed on the fence for another 8 seconds. Words came out of my mouth without thinking, "Is that you dad?" I don't believed that way but that's what happened.

The next story is so unusual so I wanted to included it in this writing.

The Cheyenne were having a run from Fort Robinson to Montana and were stopping at Oglala. My cousin Betty Sanders and I share the same great grandmother Sara Log Chin. Sara was a Northern Cheyenne who was married to David Talton Gillispie.

Betty wanted to help feed the Cheyenne so I got some food together and left Rapid headed for Oglala. I stopped at Red Shirt Table to visit my cousin Jerry Two Bulls.

As we were standing outside there were four golden eagles circling, coming from the East. The eagles got above us and continued circling. Three bald eagles came from the East a little lower than the golden eagles. Then a golden eagle and a bald eagle got in a fight almost directly above us.

Maybe things like this happen all the time I thought this to be very unusual and glad we got to see it.

The next I thought about it for quite a while before writing about my cousin Orville Two Bulls.

Orville told this story to my brother Johnnie Swallow who told me more than twenty-five years ago. Unfortunately both have passed on quite a while ago.

Orville was a policeman in Manderson, South Dakota. Orville was living with his in-laws when he went horseback riding. He was coming back and he had to ride through a stand of cider trees. Orville got part way through when his horse stopped. It legs were spread and quivering and wouldn't go any further.

Orville looked to his side and he saw an old man with long white hair sitting against a dead cedar tree.

The old man was looking down at the ground then he looked up. All of a sudden the horse bolted and began running down toward a closed gate. Orville tried to stop the horse, after failing, he had to bail off the horse and it busted through the gate.

He asked everyone he came in contact with if they knew who this old man was and nobody knew.

Some time later Pine Ridge police department called Orville to come to Pine Ridge. It was during the winter and it was snowing and at night.

He said he saw a man walking beside the road. As he passed the man, the man turned and looked at Orville.

Orville knew that was the man he saw in the stand of cedar trees.

Later Orville attended a Uwipi ceremony. I won't say what happened there out of respect for the believers, but the interpretation he got of the story was Orville was the old man and would live a long life.

Within the last few months I asked my cousin in-law, Rick Sanders, if Orville told him that story. He said he did. The only difference between the stories was that the long hair was in braids.

Some years after the story, Orville was partying with some people on the dirt road from Red Shirt Table to Oglala closer to the Buffalo Gap junction. He walked away and was found months later about ten miles in some rancher's pasture. Orville had many good qualities with a good sense of humor.

These three stories show how experiences with animals can be unexplained. Although animals are less intelligent than us humans but for the most part they are more consistent and reliable.

Chapter 19

The Historic Linehan store was a strong part of the Oglala Community

My generation, from about 70 to 90 years old, have many stories about events we have witnessed, also stories about people we knew and history of certain places. Some stories are personal while others we experienced or heard about.

The following story is about someone that was a big part of the Oglala community. Others can tell a better, more in-depth story than myself but this is what I know.

John Linehan, who was Irish, had a general merchandise store down by the Oglala Dam that served the Oglala community. I wanted to get more information from other people about the store so I got in touch with Gene Linehan a twin son of John's brother George Linehan.

George had three sons; Jimmy and the twins Neil and Gene. Gene is who I spoke with. Gene said his brother Neil is still alive.

Gene told me his uncle John worked for the B.I.A. before he acquired the store and both his dad and uncle came from Massachusetts.

My mother Lizzie Two Bulls who was born in 1907 remembered the general merchandise store always being there. She was from Red Shirt and did business in Fairburn, Buffalo Gap and in Rapid City.

My father (John Swallow) was from Black Tail which is south of the (Prairie Wind Hotel and) Casino. He had many relatives around Oglala and White River and he also knew of the store.

The store stocked just about everything that people would need. Clothing of all kinds, hats, rope, bridles and food.

Gene told me that they bought their meat from Black Hills Packing Plant in quarter sections and at the store they cut their own meat.

Dad said they had a 300-head cattle unit and after talking with Gene he confirmed it.

Many people still rode horseback and had teams and wagons.

What I know of the store covers about 35 years from what I heard from my parents to my own experiences.

My father, John Swallow, was born in 1910 and he said when they were young men and if they carried a watch it was always a pocket watch. Evidently at some point they started making wrist watches for men.

Dad asked John to order a wristwatch for him. John told dad, "Next thing you know you're going to be squatting to pee." Dad thought it was coarse but funny.

My earliest memory of the store was probably in 1944 when I was five years old. The store was down by the Oglala dam. There were teams and wagons tied up and some old people sitting outside talking to one another.

I remember during that time I was afraid of old wrinkled people and stayed away.

Funny when I told my sister-in-law, Suzanne Swallow, that as a boy I was scared of old winkled people she replied, "Vic have looked in the mirror lately?" I thought that was funny!

Back to the story. When we approached the store and stopped, I saw the old people outside. Everyone else got out of the car and went into the store except me. I was scared and stayed in the car by myself.

When they came out, I was still sitting in the car crying. My mom asked me why I was crying and I told her, "I was scared of that Unci sitting there."

Gene told me the store moved away from the dam in October of 1949.

I remember there was a well up the hill from the store where people could get water and fill their water bags. The water was real cold and tasted good.

George's boys grew up with the Oglala boys and probably talk good Lakota.

One time in the late 50s my older brother John Swallow Jr. and one of my cousins and myself went to the spillway of the dam. We were probably making lots of noise especially the car. All at once out from the trees and bushes about four or five Lakota boys on horses riding bareback came charging out and headed north.

There was a white kid with them. Brother said they were all wild even the white kid. It was one of the Linehan boys.

In later years, John Linehan and his brother George hired two helpers, one was a small Lakota man whose name was Charlie Eagle Louse then later they had his son "Little Charlie" working there.

My mother's first language was Lakota and she said John and George could talk Lakota as good as she could.

Gene also told me that both John and George learned how to sign language. He said they both communicated with two older deaf Lakota men that were at the Little Big Horn Battle. One was John Sitting Bull and the other was Homer Iron Hawk.

Gene grew up in the Oglala area and knew all the old families both Indian and non-Indian in area and surrounding communities.

There are many people older than I that know the history of the communities where they live or lived that need to write down what they know. If they don't write down, these things that they know soon there will be made up stories that are not true. That is already happening within the last couple decades.

I feel the Linehans and their store were a strong part of the Oglala community and they worked hard to provide many items available to community members to purchase. They learned Lakota and sign language to communicate better with the people they served.

Both my mother and father felt the Linehans were fair, honest and well respected within the Oglala and surrounding communities.

I just want this story to be remembered because it left a positive impact on my childhood.

Chapter 20

Two Acts of Kindness

I'm thankful for this opportunity to tell these stories that I remember and so grateful that my mother was willing to pass down these stories to me.

I have been getting emails from various readers telling me thanks for writing in while others want more information. I truly appreciate the interest in these stories which all happened during a time where people were good-hearted, simple, hard working, and easy accepting of their current situation.

Some of us elders are crabby, grumbly, and have become judgmental maybe because growing up we didn't have the luxuries of indoor plumbing and other fancy electronics that are available today.

Us elders are now living in a fast-paced, ever-changing society that we don't completely understand. That makes us more confused and helpless, but that is reality for us elders.

I try real hard to remember the good times and different happenings that made an impact on me.

The following story is back when life was simple and when acts of kindness were the norm.

Around 1950 my father started going with his family to different celebrations starting with the gold discovery days in Custer.

About that time a family from Oglala came to our house in a team and wagon. I remember other people had team and wagons for hauling wood and plowing gardens while they were using theirs for traveling.

They were heading for Custer which was about 80 miles from Oglala. Their names Asa and Lizzie Walks Out.

My mother knew them and while they stopped for a break she fed them and they left for Custer.

A few days later we drove to Custer my dad went to the Rodeo and us kids went to the carnival. After awhile we went to a hill overlooking the rodeo grounds. My mother was there visiting with Lizzie Walks Out and she had a daughter about my age.

She told her daughter to go get some cold water and make Kool-Aid for these folks. I remember it was orange Kool-Aid.

To this day when I drink orange Kool-Aid I think of Lizzie who didn't have much but was willing to share a cold drink.

I have good feelings toward that family yet still to this day.

I found out in later years the girl that served us Kool-Aid was named Norma and I talked to her about four or five years ago. She told me her own story.

Norma said after the celebration, they left and headed back to Oglala and their horses got sick. They stopped in Fairburn and stayed with Myrtle Hudspeth-Stowe who put them up for several days while her husband, Perry Stowe, doctored up the horses.

Norma said that with gratitude!

Her mother, Lizzie Walks Out, was a strong woman who did best she could to provide a good life for her kids.

My feeling is that most of the Lakota people born in the early 1900s were good, caring people who were willing to share and had many reasons to be bitter and hateful, but accepted a life of poverty and lived it and did their best with dignity.

Chapter 21

Uncle John Two Bulls

I've tried to write about people or happenings that made an impression me. The following is a story about my uncle John Two Bulls. He was born either 1897 or 1898 and the fourth child of Fred and Mary Alice One Crow-Two Bulls.

Uncle John was married the first time to a southern Cheyenne woman who died. His second marriage was to Goldie Conquering Bear. She died from several strokes before she was 50 years old.

Many people died back then. Their bodies couldn't handle the new diet of starchy, sugary, salty foods and processed meat.

My father's grandmother was a Northern Cheyenne named Sarah Long Jaw who married an Irishman named David Talton Gillispie from Missouri. She is listed in the Crazy House Surrender Ledger as Mrs. Gillispie.

When I would see Uncle John he would say, 'How is the sheyla doing today ho-kugh pee-me-chee tout-nee hobbaaceeba oba-houn-nee.' He said this so many times I can say it to this day.

My aunt, Etta Young Man, who was Long Jaw's granddaughter, used to go to Montana to see her relatives. So when she was in the hospital a Cheyenne lady came to see her. I also went up to see her as well.

I thought this was my chance to find out what Uncle John, who was once married to a Cheyenne woman, would say long ago.

I repeated it to the Cheyenne lady and she asked me to repeat it twice. She said that's not Cheyenne the guy was probably making up words.

I really did think what Uncle John had said to me was real Cheyenne words. Uncle John was a real Lakota and my dad John Swallow was a mixed blood less than half Indian. They were best friends both with strong Christian beliefs.

One time my brother John Jr., Uncle John, and my dad and I went to the badlands in my dad's jeep. My dad took his gun and went over the hill while the rest of us looked for pretty rocks.

My dad came back and said he killed a nice buck and to help him drag it back. He gutted out, and built a fire in the creek bed and roasted some flank meat and ate it with our lunch.

Uncle John asked dad if he could have some liver. Dad said have as much as you want. Uncle John took his pocket knife out grabbed a small fist size piece of liver put in it his mouth and cut the excess liver off and that's how he ate it.

In later years I thought that is all that is left for the most part of the old way of life. When we roamed free and took care of ourselves.

Uncle John was always the first to go swimming as soon as the ice melted and the water was still cold. He would head for the river with a towel over his shoulder whistling.

One year my cousins, Verdell and Delbert Yellow Horse, my brother and I decided to beat Uncle John first to swim. We stood on the bank arguing who should go in the water first. When someone pushed Verdell in, well it was me, he stood in water close to waist deep crying.

I told him to stop crying and he was first to swim and had beat Uncle John and he was the champ.

He said he was going to tell his mom on me. His parents lived a little more than a city block from us. As we were walking back he started to cry again when he was about 100 feet from the house.

After a bit, Aunt Delphine came out and looked toward our house with her hands on her hips. I avoided going by her house for several days.

I went and chopped an arm full of wood and brought it to her. She just smiled and nodded. She knew what a crazy mischievous kid I was.

I believe all of Uncle John's relatives loved him.

As an adult Uncle John would tell the little boys that would come to see him, "What the hell do you want," then proceed to tell how he was going to beat up their dad. Then later when he would go to their house he would deny saying that.

He passed away during the time I was in the Navy. Uncle John Two Bulls never lived a long time about 65 years. More of us are living into our 70's and early 80's. He had many good qualities; honest, humble and kind to name a few. I will always remember him.

Chapter 22

The Wilson Brothers 1

My stories are about people that lived in the Red Shirt Table area—stories my parents told me and what I know personally.

This story is about the Wilson Boys, Charles, whose nickname was Blooch, and Frank are the men I knew.

Blooch had hands the size of a bears paws and a nasal talk. He was a very entertaining guy who did things out of the ordinary.

Frank was a big cattle man.

This is their story. Wilson brothers were born around the turn of the 19th century. They had some Indian blood as their father was a white man and their mother was part Indian.

Mother talked about a building on the flat at Red Shirt Table. They would have white dances. Her bother Ed played the fiddle—kinda crude she said.

The Wilson boys would ride over to the dance. It was Blooch, Frank and their younger brother Owen who was just a boy. Maybe there were other boys; she never said.

Mother said her sister Dora and her had fun dancing with Owen.

Blooch was one I knew best. He lived about one mile south from my parents house in Luke Poor Thunder's log house. He lived with a hillbilly woman who everyone called "Blondiee". Blooch said she was a hillbilly and to get her to wear shoes he put dirt in her shoes.

Booch was an old cowboy who belonged to the Rodeo Cowboys Association, I think it was called. He was still bull dogging when he was in his mid 50s.

An old rancher who had a ranch east of New Underwood told me in 1971 that Blooch had a corral built West of the Fish Hatchery in Rapid City. When tourist would gather he would get his old wild horse from the bottom of the hill and charge them .25 to see him ride that horse.

There are endless stories about Blooch around the area from Rapid City to Oelrichs and all the little towns in between.

My cousin, Maurice Twiss, said Booch was in the cafe in Buffalo Gap when he was young. Blooch came in with his dog and ordered two hamburgers one cooked and the other raw. When they brought the hamburgers he gave the cooked one to his dog and he ate the raw one.

My father told me about the Two Bulls boys branding and Blooch came riding up on his horse from the west. The oldest boy, Stern, said to Blooch, "Here comes old buffalo snorts at his nuts." My dad said Blooch had a big grin on his face.

Blooch passed away at the Hot Springs V.A. That's what my dad said. My mother said he was about 60 years old in 1957. She also thought he served in World War I and II.

Frank was a big time cattleman and he would stop by in his jeep pickup and visit my dad. He was kinda big round the middle and wore suspenders and his pants were tucked in his boots. He had a gold tooth and wore a cowboy hat.

One time when he was going to brand he asked me and my brother John to help with the branding at a cow camp at the base of the west side of Cuny Table. He hired some boys from Oglala to help about six of them.

My brother said to me these guys are "Real Indians" they were polite, laughed a lot, and knew nothing about rassling calves.

They had a white kid that was staying with one of their families and his name was Clare Courtney. My brother teased him saying, "You are here after our Indian girls and when you leave there will be a bunch of yellow kids."

I told Clare if you are writing a book and if I am in the book, I want part of the money.

We showed them how to handle calves and started branding about seven in the morning and finished about five in the evening.

We branded about 1600 heads of calves.

Frank had a daughter that showed up in a T-Bird, I believe it was, and he told the guys that were branding to brand fourty heifers calves in his daughters brand.

The Wilson boys knew how to get along with Lakota people from Red Shirt to Oglala. I never heard a bad word from the real Indians about the Wilson boys. They treated those less fortunate with respect a lesson we all can learn from.

Chapter 23

My Role Model, Mark Brave

Having just had my 78th birthday and thinking about others who were of my generation are all passing away. I look back on people I knew of and I feel very fortunate to be here. Knowing life is short and uncertain, I don't want to waste time writing about petty things that really don't matter like the State and Tribal, which I believe are corrupt mess our government is in including Federal to some point.

I am grateful I am doing ok. I stay positive and write stories about people I witnessed with good hearts and who believed in themselves and worked hard, did good deeds and were successful.

I left Red Shirt Table in 1960 and joined the Navy and never went back to live there. After serving in the Navy I joined the Bricklayers Union in Rapid City in 1966 working as an apprentice.

This story begins after 1966. I was twenty-seven years old when I was working on a big job at the airport. The superintendent was an Indian guy who looked like an Indian who was a big guy. His name was Mark Brave who told me he was from Rosebud and his name was Brave Boy. He was about fifteen years older than I.

When you work for businesses in the private sector you have to compete for your job and Mark did just that.

He talked to architects, engineers and the foreman of the subcontractors and made everything come together and run smoothly.

Foreman liked working on his jobs because he had a high quality of expectations. His foundations varied no more than 1/4 inch.

Mark was a very good superintendent who showed no favoritism and was fair and very well respected in the construction industry. He worked for Hackett Construction Company which is one of the oldest construction companies in Rapid City.

He was my role model. I wanted to be like Mark who was good at his craft and respected by his fellow workers.

As I drive around Rapid City, I am reminded of all the buildings Mark worked on and showed what a good representative of Lakota people he was.

Mark and I knew each other well enough to greet each other by first name.

He was also in a band with other craftsmen and I heard they were good. Now it has been over 50 years since I worked with Mark and still think often about not only the impact he had on me, but with how he made a difference in our community as a Lakota representative.

I believed Mark lived to be about ninety years old. He was one of many Lakota people who did well in life and needed to be acknowledged!

Chapter 24

People Long Gone But Not Forgotten

I have met many people in my life time and I wanted to mention a couple for their accomplishments and stories they told me so no one is forgotten.

Victor Swallow
U.S. Navy, 1960-1964.

This happened after I served in the Navy and was discharged in December of 1964. I moved to Rapid City and started working as a laborer till May of 1966 when I got apprenticeship in the bricklayer's union.

Working gave me more money to party on. I continued this for four years.

I would go to Hermosa bar on Saturday and would sit there all day drinking. I visited with two older men. One man I knew before I went in the service; his name is Jack Zasadil. He said he was from Austria.

Jack was a very talented man. He owned a rock shop where he polished agates and sold other things. I had visited his store at one time and I remember seeing a plaque on the wall stating that he was a master gun smith.

Jack had told me he could make parts for any gun that was brought in. He also made violins. I saw one in his store he made with a lion's head carved on the stem. It was beautiful to see the work that he put into it.

He told me he worked on the carving of Mount Rushmore but he didn't go into details. He also mentioned Crazy Horse Monument and how he thought the out-stretched arm would collapse under its own weight, which made sense to me.

In 1997 I was working for West River Masonry who was doing all the masonry work for Mount Rushmore. When I was there working I saw a plaque showing names of all the men who worked there. As I read the names I saw Jack Zasadil's name.

My daughter always edits my stories and she "Googled" Jacks name and on artssouthdakota.org website Hermosa had an art show honoring his work of hand carved violins. The website showed a picture of Jack and said his first name is Johannes and he was born in 1901. He immigrated to the United States as a child.

It also said he learned how to carve violins from his uncle who was trained in Austria.

I wish I had learned of this event, I would have loved to attend and see more of his work. I enjoyed visiting with Jack and he was a very nice man.

The second man's name I remember was Al Sattler. Al loved boose more then I did. He spent a lot of time in the bar. He said he was originally from Chicago. He was apprentice mortician at the mortuary that handled the victims of the Saint Valentine's Day Massacre. He was scared of living in Chicago and moved to South Dakota.

He lived with a lady who owned a grocery store named Alice Edwards. She was a very nice lady who extended credit to Lakotas from Red Shirt Table. She told me that most of the Lakota people always settled up their debts.

Al was a harmless decent guy.

I loved that party life and had a good job and a future. I didn't appreciate it at the time. Now I own everything I did during that time.

If I could live my life over, I would do things differently.

As a Lakota, I understand addictions and make no judgements. Life can be good if you get control of your life.

Chapter 25

Comes Again High Eagle

(Boys at the Battle of Greasy Grass,
also known as Little Big Horn)

Before reservations were created, the Lakotas were nomadic. They lived off the land, dwelled in tipis, hunted buffalo, picked berries, and dug up roots. During that time the Lakota people took care of themselves and their young, always planning for the future whether they were drying buffalo meat or making dried berry patties for the winter. Decision were always made with consideration for the young and old and how each choice will affect their future.

I have two short stories about two Lakota men named Jim Comes Again and Joe High Eagle.

My mother told me when both were boys, about the ages ten or eleven, they were at the Battle of Little Big Horn in 1876. Both boys lived to be more than 80 years old.

Jim was my mother's uncle, we called him grandpa Jimmy (Kaakaa Jimmy). Later in life, I was around Grandpa Comes Again and he was a little old humped over man with skinny braids.

My brother John Swallow Jr. told me when he was ten years of age, they were butchering and Grandpa Comes

Again was overseeing the butchering. My brother said he pinched the skin on the neck of the cow and cut the jugular vein. He then cut the liver out and squeezed some bile on it and ate some of it.

A storm was coming from the west and would be there less than a hour. Butchering takes at least a few hours and a rain storm would make things harder.

Grandpa Comes Again took what my brother said looked like a soft stone maybe clay he thought out from his pocket and put it into his mouth. He chewed it and put the spit onto the inside of his arms from the elbow to his wrists.

He then prayed making parting motions with his arms towards the incoming storm.

When my brother told me this story, he was only ten and didn't say if the storm parted or not. I just remembered him telling me that story.

Later my cousin, Ed Two Bulls Jr., who was about nine years old at the time, told me Grandpa Comes Again and Joe High Eagle were two old men then and they were sitting on the ground in the shade with sticks in their hands.

It was years after the Battle of Little Big Horn and they were drawing diagrams in the dirt with their sticks showing where Custer's men were and where they were at when they were attacked.

My grandmother, Mary Alice One Crow-Two Bulls, who was Comes Again's sister-in-law, was a few years younger than both men and was listening to them. After a bit she walked through their diagram dragging her feet showing them that she was not impressed.

Joe High Eagle was not my relative so I did not hear much about him and I was never around him. I remember going to a rodeo where his grandchild was graduating. I never did see him there.

My Grandpa Comes Again served as a scout for the U.S. Army and in later years drew a scouts pension.

In the old days there wasn't many stress factors back then like we have now with worries about making ends meet and alcohol and drugs weren't an issue.

These old Lakotas had their own beliefs before Europeans forced their own religion and beliefs onto them. They were all reserved, polite and respectful which are good traits all of us should strive to be.

Chapter 26

Memories of Range Days

Summer is over the kids are back in school and the weather is changing. The Central States Fair is the last event of the summer. I think back to when I was a boy when the fair was called Range Days.

I believe my father's family started coming to the fair about 1951. We were the only one's from Red Shirt that came to Range Days Fair in the early 1950s. Later on there were a few that went to the fair.

The following stories I remember are about the fair. Some of these stories are funny, at least to me. The talk at one of the fairs was a guy who's name, I won't mention, was drunk, got on the ferris wheel, got sick and threw up on the people below him.

My dad, John Swallow, would go to the rodeo while us kids would be at the carnival. For at least five hours my brother Johnny Swallow was very good at playing the cranes where you would crank it real fast and get to swinging then drop it on silver dollars. I remember one year he came home with six silver dollars.

We would also go to the grandstand thinking we could sneak in since the rodeo was already going. There was nobody standing taking tickets. So we went in and sat down watching the rodeo. After a while a guy came and asked us for our stubs. I looked at him and said, "We don't smoke!" He asked again and I said, "I told you we don't smoke!" He run us out of there.

Sometime in the early 70s my cousin, Todd Fast Wolf, who was a big man 6'8", was at this game where you used a maul and hit this pad sending something up a shaft and ringing a bell. Todd was half shot and boasting loudly saying he was going to break the thing. A crowd gathered to see what this big loud guy would do. During his wind-up he broke wind real loud. He put the maul down and walked off.

Us Lakota men always like to wear cowboy gear. The men talk rodeo and how they were going to enter up at the coming rodeo. Steve Red Bow, besides being a World War II hero, was a good saddle bronc rider. He told his brother in laws, Pete Two Bulls's boys at the Range Days that they would see him in the arena.

He was right!

He got thrown in jail on public intoxication and when the rodeo got to the bull riding the jail birds would come out and drive steel posts and put up snow fence to make the arena smaller. Everyone had a good laugh, even Steve.

Now I am approaching 80 and going down to the fair is not as appealing to me like when I was younger. Now I hear stories from my kids and grandkids about what happened at the fair. I am content on knowing my "Range Days" are over.

The names I remember that were in the rodeo were Jack Bush Balm, Jim Shoulders, Pine Ridge's own Chet Janis and Blooch Wilson. Life back then was so simple with no television and electricity. Just radio. It was good!

Looking back, it seemed to me that we, as a people, had respect for each other.

Chapter 27

A Lakota Celebration

As I get older I have learned to appreciate gatherings more and more especially since many elders in the local communities are passing. I value the times where people get together and visit friends and family.

On Sunday, September 10th we celebrated the 79th birthday of a Lakota elderly woman who has been a strong pillar of the Red Shirt community for many decades. Because of her humble traits, I will not mention her name.

The celebration took place in Red Shirt at the arbor that was built by the Los Angeles Episcopal Church's youth group and spearheaded by Robert Two Bulls Jr., along with his father and his family.

Michael Cunningham was head of the youth group during that time the arbor was built. He and his group has done so many things for the Red Shirt community over the past decade and I am so grateful for that.

Being at the celebration brought a smile to my face as I see people arriving greeting one another with handshakes and hugs and smiles on their faces. In the background playing their guitar's and singing were Louie

Arguello and Terry Holiday consisting of their band named "Prairie Dust."

I joke around and said, "Prairie Dirt."

They have played for years at many of our gathering from birthday celebrations to the "The Great Wahampi Cook-off" and play songs of Johnny Cash and country rock music.

The people began caring their prepared food and placing it on the serving table. The serving table was about twenty-five feet long. It was full of five different soups including beans, menudo, dried meat and turnip soup, along with salads like macaroni salad, taco salad and fruit salads. Fried chicken, bbq chicken and fried bread were the finger foods.

At the end of the table were the drinks of fresh lemonade, punch and hot coffee.

As long as I could remember since I was a boy all Lakota gatherings, whether it was a funeral or a celebration, coffee was always there.

Before we ate, a Blessing was said over the food and all the people who gathered together consisted of community members, friends and family to celebrate a Lakota elderly woman's birthday.

The birthday woman went through to dish up followed by elders and the rest of the people. The whole arbor was filled with people laughing and talking and sharing each other's lives with one another.

After everyone finished eating it was time for her to open her presents. Mostly the women gathered around in a circle around the birthday woman to see each present she opened.

Birthday cards were passed around for each person to read. The birthday woman was very grateful for not only the gathering and wonderful dinner, but the heartfelt presents each family had given her.

The celebration was coming to an end and people brought out their leftover containers to fill with food and take home.

We all gathered together to celebrate this Lakota elderly woman's birthday and to show her how much we appreciate her in our lives.

She is a strong Lakota woman who had open heart surgery four months ago, lost her husband within the last four years, and was helping to raise four grandchildren.

She has many Lakota family values and displays them in her daily life and expresses those values at community meetings.

I was touched by all the events that took place at that gathering and so proud to be a Lakota.

Chapter 28

Acts of Kindness

Everyday I am reminded of all the turmoil in the world through different medias such as television and the newspapers. It is hard to stay positive when you hear such cruelty happening, but I am going to write about three stories about people I know who are making a difference in a positive light.

They don't do these good deeds to get monetary gain or acknowledgment they do it because it needs to be done. They step up with their kind hearts and open their lives to helping others.

The first story is about a two elderly Lakota ladies that live on Red Shirt Table on the Pine Ridge Reservation. One is 77 years old and the other is 79 and together they made quilts for the veterans who live at the veterans home in Pine Ridge.

At the time there were ten veterans in the home and they made each one a quilt in the memory of "Their relatives who served their country."

When I asked if I should mention their names and they said, "Maybe not." This is an example of kindness just for the sake of doing good and not wanting to be recognized. They have my deepest respect.

The next story is about two Lakota ladies from the Cheyenne River Reservation. The first Lakota woman is 76 years old and from White Horse.

When the demonstration was taking place in North Dakota, she roasted several turkeys and took them up there to help feed people. When there was a funeral, wake or special gathering, her and her family would be the first to help set up for the event, help prepare food, and stay to clean up.

She never asks for anything for her kindness and I appreciate her and all that she does.

The other Lakota lady lives in Eagle Butte. She is 75 years old and when my wife and I would stop in to see her, she always has a big pot of coffee on and something to eat.

People are always stopping in and she serves them food and coffee along with a smile, good stories that make you laugh, and her door is always open. She is always helping with special events by preparing food.

All three stories are about Lakota women in their 70s who still continue in their retirement to make a difference within their communities.

I am proud to personally know these women and want to acknowledge them not by name, but by the good deeds they do just out of the kindness of their hearts.

When I think about them a feeling of goodness overwhelms me!

The last story that more elderly are familiar with because it is about the Sioux San C.H.R. (Rapid City hospital).

Twice a year the C.H.R. has special dinners for all of the elderly. One is in the Summer where they have a BBQ at a park and serve us elderly a meal and their drivers. They provide door prizes for the elderly.

The big one is during the holiday season, a Christmas dinner. They have it at Mother Buttler Center. The tables have beautiful center pieces and they had a traditional drum group sing some songs for us.

They cook and serve a meal of turkey, ham, mashed potatoes with veggies, soup and cake and pie. They pray for us and everyone is happy and thankful for what they do for us.

Door prizes are given out and the room is filled with smiles and laughter.

My wife and I always look forward to these special events because we get to visit and feel special. Some of us won't be here next Christmas but we enjoyed the last Christmas dinner.

This is my heartfelt thank you to all involved. These two special events that make us feel special.

I hope for all good health and all the Blessing of life!

Chapter 29

Grateful for the Programs that the Democratic Party Enacted

The many times I've wanted to write to a newspaper in the last 20 years and join the hate mongers, winers, sanctimonious Christians who are sitting on their judgmental perches and the scare and doom doctors, but instead I'm going to write about positive things that happened in my family's life.

This story is about all the programs that were established by the Government over the years to help the common good of the people. Not only did I take advantage of the benefits from these programs, but so did my family.

My father, John Swallow, was in the Civilian Conservation Corps (C.C.C.) that was established by President Franklin D. Roosevelt during the Great Depression. My dad worked in camps during that time working on environmental conservation projects.

When the economy was so bad, dad said they paid him a dollar a day, which included room and board, and fortunately that was enough for them to survive.

When I think about my parents and siblings, all six of us drew from Social Security and three of us benefited from Medicare.

The G.I. bill has helped some of my cousins learn a trade so they can get a head in the world.

I personally benefited from unemployment insurance, workman's comp as well as Davis Bacon Act, which allowed the Government to pay good wages for people who were working on public work buildings.

As a Native American, a veteran, and a lifetime member of the bricklayers union, I want to publicly thank the Democratic party for enacting these programs that I utilized to look after my family.

I was able to buy a home that is now paid for and I get a union pension. Life is ok.

I am aware that the way I was raised gave me a good start at life with a father that was good at gardening, hunting, trapping, and managing his money well. He was always thinking ahead.

I know that others are struggling to survive. We live in a society that has unfortunately taken a turn for the worse but if we just keep our heads up, with a positive attitude, and try our best things will get better! Life can be ok.

I often wonder how our world would be if we didn't have these programs that truly help the greater good of the people of America.

Chapter 30

We Have Become a Country with no Conscious, Guilt or Shame

I had said in the past that I'm staying out of topics of religion and politics to write about because people have their minds made up. Most people won't change looking at religion realistically.

Jews prayed to be saved, and the people responsible for the destruction of six million Jews were worshipping the same God, which never made sense to me.

In politics the republican tribe is led by a person who is showing us he has no good qualities. His party talks about taking the country back. Our President wanted to make America great again!

I am thinking back to the 1800s when slavery and manifest destiny was the rule of the country. The really disturbing thing about the whole mess is that our elected representatives support the decisions that have been made and unfortunately our country is headed back to the mentality of the 1800s.

Respect for the United States of America has been lost from nearly all of the world with the exception of Russia and other countries with dictators. The last straw for me is when our President signed the defense bill that was named after John McCain, a prisoner of war, and he didn't mention it was made for him.

Our President doesn't have no respect for our military heroes which is one of many things I don't agree with.

As a Native and a Veteran who served my country along with others who feel things in the government are getting out of control, we need to try to change things in South Dakota. It seems hopeless like calling for help during a raging blizzard or a salmon trying to swim up Niagara Falls.

Many of us Native veterans gave part of our lives to make this country safe, a good place to live, respect for one another, and other countries.

Coming from a warriors society, we served a country that did much evil to our own people.

The only way we can change things is by taking interest in the coming election and voting.

I know many of us have relatives and others you know who are eligible to vote but haven't taken any interest or don't have the means to get registered. Don't waste your time talking to member of the republican tribe.

I might be the only one that thinks this way, but it is real. But if there are others who feel the same way I do then if we all band together and we can try to make a difference in the coming election.

Make an effort to talk to your relatives and anyone you know and tell them what is happening with all the bills coming up to vote. Enlighten them about the representatives and what they stand for and their past track records.

Evidently our fellow South Dakota representatives love their Republican party more than the common good of our country. We can try to change things in our own neighborhood in the state of South Dakota.

We have become a country with no conscious, guilt or shame.

Chapter 31

The Unexpected Destruction of Their Way of Life

Most of what I write about are people that lived in the Red Shirt Table and Oglala area where I lived till 1960.

My mother, Lizzie Two Bulls, talked a lot to me and my older brother, John Swallow II. We paid attention and asked questions and in later years I started to write down what my mother told me. I will continue to share these stories.

This next story is about three Lakota men that my mother knew that lived through an ever changing era from roaming free and hunting to the Government killing all the buffalo to the Little Big Horn Battle in Montana in 1876.

They experienced the Ghost Dance that came about that brought hope to the Lakota people of a returning nomadic lifestyle.

They also lived through the Wounded Knee Massacre in 1890 where they knew about the slaughter of their elders, their women and their children.

These old Lakota men were at the Little Big Horn battle all were in the Manderson and Holy Rosary Mission area at the time of the Wounded Knee Massacre.

My grandfather, Fred Two Bulls, was at Holy Rosary Mission. He was twenty years old and his first child was born there 18 days after the Wounded Knee Massacre.

He never said whether he believed in the Ghost Dance but he did go to prison. Mom said some place in Indiana and from there to Europe performing in the Wild West Show.

The Government started enrolling natives. They were given first names. They asked one old fellow what name he wanted, and he said, "Jesus." They said he couldn't have that name, and asked what other name and he said, "Mary."

Many Lakotas from that time till now have Biblical first names. I don't know what name he ended up with.

Mom talked about brothers named Drags Rope, Mountain Sheep and Wilson Knee. In later years I did find out what Drags Rope's first name is Joe.

I went to a museum in Timber Lake where there was a display of a gadget to start fire that was given to a Mrs. Laplante known as "Wincincala" by her cousin Joe Drags Rope. The curator of the museum, a nice guy, named Jim Nelson, told me that Joe Drags Rope wasn't a Cheyenne River name.

My mother told me sometime in the 1920s a Mrs. Laplante, who had one blue eye, also had a little boy named Victor who came to visit her cousin, Mountain Sheep.

I found a later account of Drags Rope in a biography of Custer. I read that in the book The Son of the Morning Star by Evan S. Connell. It mentions an account of a lost breadbox given by an Oglala named Drags Rope in 1939.

My mother told me the men she knew were at the Battle of Little Big Horn were High Eagle, Drags Rope, and Jim Comes Again, who was also known as Bear Comes Growling. They were young men.

I assume that Mountain Sheep and Wilson Knee was also their because they were Drags Rope brothers but mother never mentioned that.

All these men lived their childhood roaming free, hunting, and preparing for winter. They celebrated victory when attacked by a source much smaller than they were. They witnessed broken treaties and the destruction of the buffalo which was their lifeline and their way of life.

The Ghost Dance movement came and gave them hope that their old way of life would return and also the Europeans would be gone.

The Wounded Knee Massacre happened and their hopes were shattered and spirits broken.

Realizing you can't win against a people that disarms you and kills old men, women and children. They outlawed their most sacred ceremony, the Sun Dance.

My grandpa, Jimmy Comes Again, was last of the wild ones and a scout before the Wounded Knee Massacre and he never forgot the destruction of his old life.

Mom said it was rumored Jimmy evened things up when he came on a lone white man.

In the later years of his life he was a little humped over man with skinny braids. He drew a scout's pension.

I believe he passed away in the late 1940s.

These men in that generation had their lives turned upside down. They had that lost feeling with no hope. They survived through it all eating horse meat, prairie dog, roots, berries and rations from the Government.

We are a broken people and most of us wouldn't know how to survive without the help from the same Government that destroyed our ancestors ability to take care of themselves.

Things have to change, but where to start?

Now we are here with all our problems. It's said Little Wolf of the Cheyenne people prayed at Bear Butte, "Great Spirit hear me, the people are broken and scattered. Let the winds bring a few seeds together that we may grow strong again in a good place."

The question is where do we start.

Chapter 32

Thin Milk

(The end of the Ghost dancers' Dream;

Asanpi Bleza-Thin Milks Death—a Forgotten Warrior)

The story begins in 1948 with John Swallow and his boys, Johnny age twelve and Victor age nine, and also their uncle John Two Bulls going into a canyon between Red Shirt and Blindman Table. They were going to look at human remains that John Swallow had found. The story ends 113 years later in 2003 with a Lakota ceremony that put this persons spirit to rest.

In the years after the breaking of the 1868 treaty that shrank of the Great Sioux Reservation then occurred Little Big Horn Battle, killing of Crazy Horse, and the buffalo were gone. The Lakota were confined to small reservations completely dependent on the U.S. government for staples to keep them alive.

In 1890 beef rations for the Rosebud Brulés were cut to two million pounds and the Oglala by one million pounds. They were a people whose former way of life was destroyed. They were destitute. Lost with no hope for tomorrow.

Furious.

Along came this movement from Utah, the Great Dance. If they did this dance a certain way, and also other things their former life would return to following the buffalo herds, preparing for winter by drying meat, berries, and roots, and the Europeans would be gone.

This movement swept through the reservations. Asanpi Bleza was part of this movement.

The Rosebud Brulés were headed toward Pine Ridge laying waste and helping themselves to everything in their path. They ended up at the stronghold—a natural fortress that could easily be defended.

From there, raiding parties went out to ranches bordering the reservation in search of food and also some senseless destruction above their needs.

The story of Thin Milk's death is a story told to me and my siblings by our mother, Lizzie Two Bulls Swallow who was born in 1907. She was the second generation out of the wild. Her grandparents were born out on the prairie somewhere.

Mother was interested in history. She told of many events that happened in her early life.

Thin Milk was part of a raiding party from the stronghold. They went to the Daley Ranch and were surprised by returning cowboys who shot Thin Milk. His fellow warriors carried him across the Cheyenne River and up the Cedar Creek canyon where he told them to leave him and to come back later.

When they came back he was dead. Mother said it was winter time—sometime around the Wounded Knee Massacre.

Then when mother was a girl, Thin Milk's people came looking for his remains. She said they were Rosebud Indians and offered a hundred dollars to anyone who found Thin Milk's remains.

A man whose name was Wilson Knee searched the canyon for many days. Then, I believe it was in 1948, my father who was part of a Cattlemen's Association, was out riding when he found Thin Milk's remains.

He took us boys and Uncle John down there in a 1947 jeep that he bought as a demonstrator.

The remains were the skull cap and smaller bones. Uncle John built a wooden box and he told dad he buried them somewhere close by the spot where Thin Milk's remains were found.

Sometime in the middle of the 1990s, my brother started saying we have to do something about Thin Milk before we die.

There were only three of us who knew where his remains were, who had found them, and knew the complete story. Our father was eighty-five years old and not as sharp as he used to be.

We talked about it many times, about the Ghost Dancers, their beliefs, how a people with no hope whose livelihood and their way of life was gone forever. They accepted the movement with the belief their former life would return.

It was my brother's passion to acknowledge Thin Milk's death and tell the story our mother Lizzie Two Bulls Swallow told us about Thin Milk.

John L. Swallow II, U.S. Army 1960-1966.

In 2000, brother went to the edge of the Badlands and put up a steel column with a pipe attached to it. He went down into the canyon and put up a marker at the approximate spot where Thin Milk's remains were found.

Shortly thereafter, I poured a piece of concrete with his name and approximate date of his death. Also, the story was put on cedar planks telling the basic story—all this on the edge of the Table.

We talked about a simple ceremony since markers were in place. Then, I talked to a lady from the Rapid City Journal and they printed the story. Cousin Robert Two Bulls suggested a Thin Milk ride. He would get his brother, Sam Two Bulls, to do a ceremony for Thin Milk.

The Thin Milk ride was born on the morning of the third Sunday of September 2003. After a blessing and smudging of the riders and horses by Philomine Lakota. Thirty-five riders, Lakota and non-Lakota, rode off retracing Thin Milk's last ride. It was led by Robert Two Bulls and Paul Hava, who was leading a two-year-old appaloosa stud with a bright red blanket on.

They came up the canyon with many people watching from the edge of the Table. When they reached the site of Thin Milk's remains, Layo Robert Two Bulls said a prayer.

Then from the Table, I called Thin Milk's name, Asanpi Bleza, over the canyon four times. Philomine Lakota talked and sang a song.

Then Sam Two Bulls did a Lakota ceremony and prayer for Thin Milk's spirit. A drum group from Porcupine (I believe the Thunder Hawks) just showed up and sang a song for Asanpi Bleza.

Finally, a 113 years after his death, brother Johnny's passion was complete. Asanpi Bleza's life and death was acknowledged. (*Sign by Victor and John.*) His spirit was set free. Two months after the second ride, brother passed on.

Again, on the morning of the third Sunday in September 2008, the ride by Robert Two Bulls family and the Swallow families was organized to acknowledge the life and death of a Lakota Ghost Dancer began the fifth time.

(A story as told by Lizzie Two Bulls Swallow and sons John Swallow Jr. and Victor Swallow.)

Chapter 33

Thoughts on Aging

I haven't been up to writing lately for many personal reasons. I am going to write about old age and experiencing getting older. As a kid I use to be afraid of old people.

I remember I was about five years old and my parents and I went to the Linehan store in Oglala on the Pine Ridge Reservation. There were some old people sitting outside the store. I was scared and didn't want to walk past them to enter the store so I stayed in the car and cried. My mom asked me how come I didn't come in the store I said, "I'm scared of that unci over there."

Unci in Lakota means grandma.

Now I look in the mirror and wonder if any kids are afraid of me.

This summer I turned 80 years old. As I get older I tend to stumble and walk slower and I have to be more mindful of where I plant my steps. I say huh… a lot. My mind is not very sharp and my personal appearance is not so important anymore.

I am happy to visit anyone, anywhere at anytime. Just waiting for anyone willing to give me the attention and the time. I take naps all day and can sleep at anytime.

Most of the time I am half comfortable and always living with some pain. I take a handful of pills and now I tend buy more than one bottle of prune juice at a time. I think about others that were a lot younger in my life that passed away and I am still here.

I am doing ok.

Two things the Lakota elders look forward to within this community are the elderly picnic and Christmas party the C.H.R. from Sioux San Hospital that is put on for us every year.

They treat us like we are special. My wife and I always get to the picnic early to get good seats. Generally I am the only rooster in the hen house.

I notice as the ladies walk from their cars to the picnic they are either shuffling or waddling.

One year Silas Sound Sleeper came to the picnic. I almost got up and hugged him I was so happy there were two roosters now.

Someone told me that he was in a nursing home in White River.

This last August at the picnic there was a guy by the name of Rattling Chase who was from Sioux San and I visited with him. I told him about seventy years ago there was a guy named John Rattling Chase who would ride horse back to Red Shirt village on the Pine Ridge Reservation.

People called him John Huste. I asked my mom what "Huste" means in Lakota and she said it means "lame." I found the connection between the two.

After visiting with Rattling Chase I noticed he was well versed with the past dealings with the Federal Government and the Lakotas.

I would like to list all the people who attend the C.H.R. events that I know but it wouldn't be fair to the rest of them.

I will name one who was two weeks away from her 95th birthday. Her name is Faith Babby from the McGaa family. She still drives but has a hard time getting in and out of the car.

Alton Yellow Boy was the M.C. and the prayer was by Reverend Yellow Hawk. The drum group sang a few songs and Pansy Hawk Wing sang as well.

The food consisted of sloppy joes, hot dogs, potato salad, baked beans, cake and coffee. It was real food and good!

They gave out door-prizes and had a round dance.

I want to thank several people for organizing an event that my wife and I enjoy so much over the years: Jessie Romero who started it; Sharon Lazotte for continuing it, and all the other people behind the scenes who are kind hearted to be a part of an event that make so many elderly Lakotas feel special.

Us elderly have stories to tell. Stories about the hardships we endured. Stories about our boarding school days. Some even have stories about World War II. Stories about the old Lakotas that knew what it was like to roam the wilderness and live free.

As an adult after my kids became adults and started their lives, I watched my dad with every year passing slowly losing ground. First using a cane then he was unable to live alone and moved in with my sister.

Hearing was the next to go for my dad. When he tried to gather his thoughts it took longer and soon he was using a walker

Dad was so weak soon the walking stopped and the last memories of him were being spoon fed in a nursing home by a worker.

I remember he had streams of tears running down his face as he was eating. That was a hard site to see.

I want to leave you with a thought, whether you are up in age like me or just starting a family and anywhere in between, remember life is precious and taking time to see your relatives while they are still alive is priceless.

As you get past retirement your outlook on life is different. You don't want to burden your relatives with your troubles, issues or concerns. Things that you once did easily just waits for a more able bodied person to come along and do it.

Pride gets in the way of asking others for help and the fear of hearing a "No I can't help you" is another way of rejection. So all you young able bodied people make the initiative to ask your elders if they need help because most of us won't ask you.

Chapter 34

Sometimes we Have to Make Choices for the Good of the People

I have many stories and things I've experienced that I want to share having lost my wife of 52 years to COPD complications in February. I haven't had a desire to do much of anything. The last article my daughter and I wrote dealt with my 12 day stay in the hospital from the COVID 19 virus. I struggle with many problems as a result of the virus but I'm doing ok.

Many people my age above 80 years old have stories to share which we should do or they will be lost.

Unfortunately we are still in a pandemic and we all had to learn to live with social distancing, wearing masks and self-quarantining.

The following stories are about unexpected situations told by my mother and other unfortunate experiences I know.

My mother, Lizzie Two Bulls, was born in 1907. She said they were in Pine Ridge Boarding School during the 1918 Spanish Influenza. From the school they could see the cemeteries of the Episcopal and Catholic churches. Mother said all day long for many days there where wagons hauling the dead. She said some of the girls in the boarding school got sick. Mother never said any of them died.

To avoid the spread of the Spanish Flu, they isolated the sick and had them drink lots of water and plenty of bed rest.

Mother said her older sister Lucy lost her husband to the Spanish flu. He was from Cheyenne River Agency. I believe his name was Willie Circle Eagle. He was buried in the Episcopal cemetery. I believe it was in an unmarked grave.

I was six-years-old when I went to boarding school and during that the whole time I attended I had the mumps, chicken pox and measles.

I remember the mumps were painful. I can't remember when and where I got the small pox vaccine and another shot on each arm. I have a big scar from those shots.

When I joined the Navy and was leaving for overseas I had to get eight shots.

All my children throughout their lives have been vaccinated and now as adults they have the COVID 19 vaccine.

My youngest daughter although vaccinated got the second round of COVID and she had flu-like symptoms. Her roommate who didn't get the vaccine got COVID at the same time and his symptoms were more severe and took him longer to recover.

I understand that getting the vaccine is a personal choice people make for themselves and their families. People need to look at the big picture of getting this vaccine. With the millions of millions of people who got vaccinated and some might have an adverse reaction to the vaccine. The majority of the people who got the vaccine had mild to no symptoms.

In 2004 I had a five bi-pass heart surgery. Before the surgery the heart doctor gave me a survival rate--out of 100 people there are two people that have complications from this surgery. I chose to have heart surgery adding to the quality of my life not to mention prolonging it.

Why would I make a judgement on the two percent of complications? Life is about choices and I made and continue to make my choices based on numbers.

I can't count the times that I have been vaccinated during my lifetime. What I won't do is cry around when my choices catches me.

We've had people fight the seatbelt law, no smoking in public places, and other laws that are for our own good.

I want to relate a story about my brother John Swallow Jr who was going around with a swollen jaw and told me he had a decayed tooth. He had been dealing with the pain for two weeks.

I told him go and get it pulled and he said he didn't like it when the dentist poked him with that needle. I said evidently you like the tooth ache which is a constant pain instead of the pain from the needle which is over in seconds. He said I was right.

In World War II from 1939-1945 as a country we had to rally and do our part to defend against our enemy. While the men went to war the women of our country stepped up and filled the spots in the factories. Our country's economy had to shift and we had to adjust to stipends with our fuel, food and supplies. Tokens were given out to regulate the spending and consumption.

Supplies were in shortage during the World War II and we had to adjust.

As a country we have to have a similar mind set as during World War II because we are in a war against this pandemic and we must defeat it.

Unfortunately most people can say they know of someone who had been affected by this pandemic whether they lost their job, tested positive or knew someone who died. We are not talking about other people or a different community, this is affecting our community and our people.

I was fortunate to have survived COVID 19 back in November of 2020 and I learned my lesson. I have lost three of my cousins to COVID complications and through my family I know of a handful more deaths that have affected them.

This second round of COVID is a different strand and is more contagious and is affecting our youth.

When I go out in public I wear a mask not only for my own safety but for the safety of the people around me which is my friends and family. I won't wish getting COVID on my worst enemy.

This virus is dangerous and unpredictable. It doesn't discriminate against age, color, political party, religious affiliation or economic status.

I want to be around to watch my great grand kids grow up and I will do what I can to protect them.

When the third vaccine shot comes out I will be the first in line to get it. I don't like the thought of another twelve days in the hospital away from my loved one's hooked up to an oxygen machine, or worse ending up in a very hot place.

Chapter 35

Lakota Story 3

During this time in our society where negativity seems to take the spotlight. I want to share a story told to me by my mother that shows a positive aspect of life.

My mother who was born in 1907 told me this story that happened in 1917. It is about a trip she took to Rapid City from Redshirt Table.

It took about two days with a team and wagon and along the way they stopped to relieve themselves leaving my mother's grandma who didn't speak any English at the wagon. Her name was Bird All Over. She was in her 70s.

When they all got back to the wagon she said a white man on horseback came and talked to her but she didn't know what he was saying. They asked her to remember one word the man said and she said, "Eat" and pointed that way.

They followed the direction the white man said and there were bushes of buffalo berries. At the time all the white people knew what the Lakota's ate.

After they arrived in Rapid City my mother's father took my mother to a Church where she sang "Onward Christian Soldier" in English and in Lakota. They gave them some money and groceries. My mother said she thought it might have been a Salvation Army Church.

Mother's parents never did learn English. My mother did her last two years of schooling at the Rapid City Indian School.

Simple stories like these told to me by my mother remind me of the simple days were gratitude was expressed daily and negative aspects just didn't exist.

I think about these stories and how a snack of buffalo berries would have been nice during a road trip and maybe on their way back they might of picked some more to dry for the winter all because a white man told them where to find them.

During that time our people who lived under a military rule with very few rights accepted it and adjusted their way of life to survive.

I encourage you to learn some of your old stories before they are gone.

Chapter 36

Remembering Our World War I and II Veterans

A holiday I always hold dear to my heart is Veteran's Day. As a Oglala Lakota raised on the Pine Ridge Reservation growing up with people who served our country, we held veterans in the highest honor.

Veteran's Day has come and gone. This year I tried to go down and see the parade but with the high wind I didn't go.

My cousin, Robert Two Bulls, who served in the Navy during the Korean War is usually with the Korean Veterans in the parade. As a veteran who served four years in the Navy, I have respect for anyone who joined and served their country.

I want to write about men that stood out in my mind who gave their lives for our country. Many of these veterans came home broken while others handled it pretty good considering they had to experience traumatic events and took human lives. I'll write a little something about each of them.

Years ago I was visiting my aunt Edna Serry and asked why her aunt Margie Gallisipie-Dreamer got married so late in life. She said the man she was supposed to marry joined the army and went to serve in World War I and got killed.

I asked her what his name was and she said she couldn't remember. About a-half-hour later I ask her again and she said it was Sam White Bear. This was during a time when Natives were not citizens of the United States of American and not allowed to vote.

The other person I know who served in World War I was Charles (Blooch) Wilson who was a rough neck. Blooch had hands the size of a bears paws and a nasal talk He was a very entertaining a guy who did things out of the ordinary.

My mother said she thought Blooch served in World War II also and would have been in his mid 40s.

I want to mention the following people by name who served in World War II:

My cousin, Earl Two Bulls, the second son of Stern Two Bulls lost his life on some island in the West Pacific.

My uncle Woodrow Swallow (born 1924) was seventeen when he joined the Navy in 1941. The way my father John Swallow tells it Uncle Woodrow's dad had to sign for him to join the Navy. Dad said, "He was just a boy," and his voice would break.

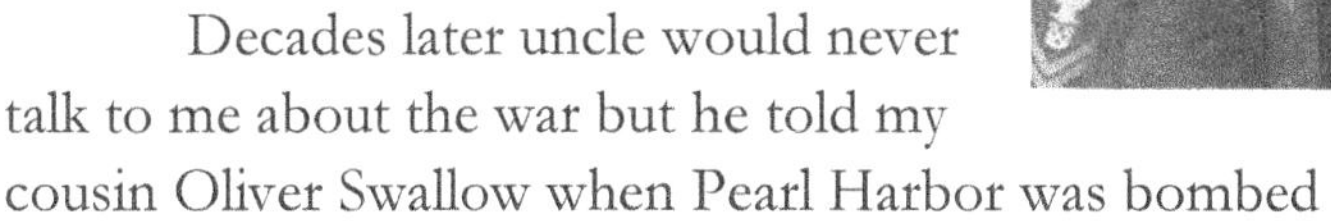

Decades later uncle would never talk to me about the war but he told my cousin Oliver Swallow when Pearl Harbor was bombed uncle Woodrow was on a ship. He saw something came rolling across the deck and it was somebody's head.

When he was discharged he came back to South Dakota and farmed and had a small herd of cattle.

Uncle Woodrow left the state in the 1950s and moved to Utah and became a certified diesel mechanic. He handled his war experiences pretty well.

Another veteran I want to honor is Pat Cuny who lived in the Red Shirt area most of his life. He served in the Army in World War II over in Europe.

Pat didn't talked much about the war but he did tell me the Russian army came to help. Pat said they had real long rifles and a big loaf of black bread and a bottle of vodka. Many of them were drunk and headed toward the Germans. His words were, "They mowed them down."

Pat lived alone never married and had no children that I know of. He was the last of the real cowboys. He lived at one time alone along the Cheyenne River on the Pine Ridge Reservation. Pat took care of cattle in the badlands.

He loved rodeos and liked a good party. When Pat passed away the services were held at the fairgrounds in Hermosa. Many people were there to pay their respects to a war hero.

Pat had a good heart and a sense of humor but with a foul mouth. A good example of his sense of humor is when my cousin Oliver Swallow's friend, who was a trucker, came up to get some buffalo meat. The trucker would cook black eyed peas with sorghum syrup and my cousin baked biscuits. Those of us that were there ate including Pat.

The next year when cousin Oliver's trucker friend came back and he cooked up the same dish Oliver called Pat and asked are you coming over to eat? Pat said, "Hell No! I am still farting from the last time I ate that stuff."

To this day when I think of Pat I remember him saying that and it still makes me laugh.

My cousin Mazie married Steve Red Bow. He was a full blood who served in the Army over in Europe. He said he was captured and they were taking them somewhere in a cattle car on a train.

Steve said it was during the winter and there was lots of snow. He and another soldier jumped out of the train into a snowbank and somehow made it to an allied camp.

Steve was injured and lost one of his kidneys and probably other internal organs. He drew some kind of a pension.

Steve was a humble caring person. He and Mazie had no natural children but adopted two children who they loved and raised. Steve functioned well and was good at basketball, baseball and a good saddle bronc rider.

Another World II vet I know but never talked to is Eddie Rooks. He would come to Red Shirt to visit his cousin Emily Janis-Two Bulls who was married to my uncle Jake Two Bulls. As I understood that, Eddie lost a leg in the war in Europe and used crutches.

He drove a fairly new car a 1949 Buick and he like to drink. My uncle Jake was thrilled when Eddie came by and they would head for town.

One story they told, Eddie drove on somebody's lawn and got stuck. They bailed out of the car and started to run down the street. Uncle said Eddie kept up with him. Eddie would fall a little behind and then lurch ahead. Uncle Jake said afterwards they had a good laugh.

There are many others that went to war and did their duty. They are all gone now and we never did enough for them. There are some I knew and others I didn't know very well.

My cousin Elizabeth was married to Ambrose Belt who was in the Navy. I found out from his daughter Mary that he fought against the Japanese. Ambrose was a humble kind-hearted man who got along with everyone. He owned horses. Some thoroughbreds that he raced.

All these men went as teenagers to serve their country without question. Then they came home with many issues but for the most part did ok.

I like to end this article with something my mother Lizzie Two Bulls-Swallow told me that stayed with me all these years. She said some Native from the eastern part of the state got killed in World War II. When they brought his body home his people wanted to bury him in Sioux City's cemetery. The city wouldn't allow it so President Truman had him buried in Arlington National Cemetery.

I wish all of the veterans that have passed on still were alive so I could shake their hand and tell them how thankful I am for their service.

I also wish I could tell them during the time they served their country and fought in the wars as a country we were united and didn't hate each other.

Back then religion had meaning and people were more patriotic. When you said the "Pledge of Allegiance" it meant something and people lived it.

Our country is far from perfect but it was a united people that had hope. Unfortunately, I can't say it's the same country with its values they fought for because of all of the hate and evil festering.

I keep thinking about when Pat Cuny told me when he was a teenager signing up for the war he said a lot of other teenagers lined up along with him.

During the World War I and II many of our men signed up as teenagers without a second thought and I think that is honorable.

I want to personally thank all of the people who enlisted to serve our country for laying their life on the line to make our country safe.

Many veterans come back physically, mentally and socially damaged and for some reason people look the other way. As a society, we seem to take veterans for granted never really realizing the sacrifices they made.

Chapter 37

A Heart Felt Tribute to Veterans

With this past Veteran's Day, I want to write first about the old Lakotas before and after the European invasion when my people were a complete and whole society. Then I want to write about experiences that were told to me and my own service in the Navy.

Before the Europeans came into our lives our warriors supplied the meat and defended us against our enemies. Our leaders and chiefs were brave men who had respect for acts of bravery, even with our enemies. We never had a chief who was a coward.

Once assimilation happened I think about when our men who were in the Armed Forces had to fight for our freedom. They didn't enjoy the same benefits as the rest of the people in our country did. Especially during World War I and II where our United States freedom was at stake.

As opposed to some of the more recent wars overseas. Our service men have fought our wars of choice. They are heroes none the less.

My grandfather, Oliver Swallow, had 12 grandsons and ten of us served our country. His youngest son, Woodrow Swallow, was 17 years old when he joined the

Navy. Grandpa had to sign for Uncle Woodrow to join. He was in Pearl Harbor when it was bombed.

I remember when my father, John Swallow, would talk about Uncle Woodrow being in Pearl Harbor and only seventeen years old he would get choked up saying, "He was just a boy."

When I joined the Navy in 1960. When I came home on leave to Red Shirt Village, people came out of their homes and lined up to shake my hand. I didn't realize how my own people felt about my service in the military and them making a point to look me in the eye and shake my hand made me feel honored.

My cousin, Robert Two Bulls, said people did the same thing for him when he came back on leave from the Korean War in the early 1950s. At the end of the people, his Grandpa Sam Helper came out of his daughter Martha's house with his drum and sang an honoring song for him. I thought that was very special.

Cousin Robert said his Grandpa Sam Helper was from the Hump family from the Cheyenne River Reservation and was born in the 1870s. I want to write my opinion and what I know about Sam.

His name originally was Hump. He could have been at Little Big Horn as a little boy.

Last year I attended a speaker, Donovin Sprague, at the Journey Museum (in Rapid City). He talked about The Battle of Greasy Grass and Little Big Horn. He mentioned Crazy Horse and Chief Hump and others too.

Sam Helper lived through some hard times and understood the meaning of being a brave warrior.

My parents moved to Red Shirt Village for four years during school in 1947-1951.

I remember hearing Sam singing at dawn and then again at dusk. I often wondered what he was singing about.

Was he singing about the past, present or future? Was it a prayer? I know it was a tradition. Still to this day I wonder what was so important that he would consistently sing at every dawn and dusk.

When I joined the Navy I was 21 and single with no children. I joined because I wanted to get off the reservation and out of South Dakota and see the world. I have ported at Japan Yokosuka, Sasebo, and Kobe, Hawaii, Philippines, and Hong Kong. I got to experience other cultures and see different landscapes.

Back in 1960s when I was in Japan I remember some Japanese people would come onto the dock and separated the steel cans, plastic, food and paper from our ship. They have no natural resources so they recycled our cans and plastics. The Japanese knew then the importance of recycling over 50 years ago.

An experience I remembered when I was on the ship, we had a band that would play the national anthem. After it played my little friend asked me, "Do you get a lump in your throat when you hear the national anthem?" I told him yes, and I still do to this day.

When I think about some of the people who serve in our Armed Forces many of them have families. When they are deployed they are away from their loved ones for months to years at a time. They miss out on the little everyday things that most of us take for granted like the first steps of your baby, attending an award ceremony of your child's accomplishment, birthdays, holidays, your spouse's promotion, and those moments that make you proud to be a parent.

So I want to take a moment to recognize the families of the people of the armed forces because they are serving in their own way. Husbands and wives are left to raise their kids alone during those times of deployment for their spouse. Kids have to deal with life with one parent.

I also think about the soldiers that served and gave up their life for our country which is an ultimate sacrifice. My heart goes out to their friends and family who lost a loved one in combat.

I also think about our veterans who come back severely injured. Others are dealing with Post Traumatic Stress Disorder (PTSD) and their lives have been altered forever.

Warriors who have served in every war from World War I to the present day can be proud of their service when others wouldn't serve. To all the veterans I say despite your current circumstances you can pound your chest with pride and say, "I did my duty!"

So now when your hear any patriotic song like the National Anthem or say the Pledge of Allegiance, remember all the things our country the United States stands for. Think about the people who serve or served in the Armed Force and their families and the ones how gave their lives for us.

I thank you for your service to all veterans! You deserve a good life! Keep your head up, there are better days ahead. My deepest respect and appreciation. Happy Veteran's Day!

Chapter 38

Honoring our World War II Veterans

(listed as Bombing Range 1 and Victor Swallow's active duty October 1960-December 1964)

I wanted to write this story about World War II veterans because we as a society never honored and showed our appreciation to these veterans as individuals and their families who supported them.

I am going to write about several different thoughts concerning World War II: the bombing area on the reservation; an account of a B-17 plane crash on a training mission; and also mention some War Veterans that I knew and or knew of.

My family lived about three miles from the west side border of the bombing area and eight-to-ten miles from where they were bombing.

I was five years old and older when I remembered the bombers flying over the area. You could see the bombs being dropped from the airplanes and hear the explosions.

The fighter planes would fly high up and dive down and shoot their 50 caliber guns in rapid fire. Dad called the bigger bullets 20 millimeters or canons which sound like "Boom boom" when they fired.

I heard the grown ups talking about Japanese prison camps and how the Japanese prisoners might escape. Every sound I would hear in the night I was sure it was one of those Japanese prisoners that had escaped. I was really scared!

Later during my first year in Boarding School in Pine Ridge, before they showed a movie they would give updates on the war.

The crash of the B-17 is my dad, John Swallows', account of what happened. He belonged to a Cattlemen Association and he was out riding checking on his cattle. He was going home riding up the eastside of Red Shirt Table when a bomber flew overhead sputtering smoking and flying lower than normal.

As it flew East past Blindman's Table he saw a man parachute out before it went out of sight. He heard an explosion and saw smoke and rode towards where he last saw the plane.

When dad got to the crash site there were other riders there. Soon after they found the man that bailed out. He had slammed into the side of a hill and he was dead. Dad said he thought the plane was to low when he jumped out.

Bauly No Neck pulled the man's shirt over his head out of respect. It was a somber scene for the riders. My cousin, Bob Two Bulls, was nine years old when this happened. He said his father, Pete Two Bulls, got some sage and chewed it to help him deal with what happened.

Cousin Bob also remembered it happened in 1944. I remembered a lot of military vehicles around the reservation. I asked cousin Bob, he said it was nine ambulances, it seemed like there was other vehicles as well.

To get to the (Ellsworth) Airbase they would have to go around Buffalo Gap because there was no bridge to cross the Cheyenne River at Red Shirt.

In 1948 dad bought a jeep. It could just about go anywhere. He took my brother Jonnny and I to the crash site in 1950. There were bits and pieces, gages, and little stuff. We saw a motor buried in the side of a hill. I was eleven years old that year.

Forty eight years later in 1998 I took my grandson out to the crash site. I remembered exactly where that motor was and he got to see it. I found a stainless steel valve. The shaft was bent and broken.

Some years back the Episcopal Church on Red Shirt Table had an honoring and memorial service for the nine men who lost their lives in that crash and all the World War II veterans invited their relatives. Cousin Bob Two Bulls said people felt sad for the loss of those men and all the veterans who gave so much.

Here are some of the World War II veterans that I knew or knew of.

First my cousin Earl Two Bulls who lost his life on some island in the West Pacific.

Second is Steve Redbow. He was a good athlete. He played basketball, baseball and was a good saddle bronc rider.

Third was my uncle Woodrow Swallow who was only seventeen years old when he was in Pearl Harbor when it was bombed.

Another, Ambrose Belt was a humble man and always had a big smile.

Pat Cuny was one of the last real cowboys.

My other uncles, Elwood and Stan Serry, Willard Cuny, and Eddie Rooks were are all heroes with good hearts and deserve to be remembered along with many others.

There are many of us veterans that served and stood ready to defend our country during peace time and these men that I knew and knew of served during war time. So if you see any veterans shake their hand and give them a pat on the back because they are willing to give their lives for our country.

Chapter 39

Things I'm thankful for This Holiday Season

My daughter Vikki Swallow, who dresses up my writings, said I ought to write about the things I am thankful for. As an older person who has seen many changes in my lifetime, I have many things to be thankful for.

What I am most thankful for is our United States programs that the government enacted during my parents generations that many of U.S. citizens utilize.

I looked back to my grandparents, Fred and Mary Alice Two Bulls. They were born in 1870 and 1871. Their way of life was completely destroyed. Their most sacred ceremonies were outlawed. The ability to take care of themselves ended with the slaughter of the buffalo and they were forced onto reservations.

They became a people with no hope who had to result to eating horse meat and drowning out prairie dogs to get fresh meat.

Despite a radical change in their lifestyle, they kept their heads up. They were proud, honest, hated no one, and through it all they raised 11 children.

When Franklin D. Roosevelt became President he created Civilian Conservation Corps (CCC) which created work programs for unemployed men to develop our natural resources on land that the local, state and federal government owned.

My father, John Swallow, worked in the CCC when a dollar a day could feed a family. Decades later my daughter Vikki at sixteen years old worked a summer in the Black Hills for Youth Conservation Corps and enjoyed that program, and made some extra money.

Former President Roosevelt also signed into law Social Security which I have been drawing since 2002.

Another bill signed by Former President Roosevelt is the G.I. Bill which allows veterans to get a college education, unemployment insurance, and housing.

Over the years I have watched veterans I know get an education and find a good paying job to support their families.

One of the last United States programs I am thankful for is Medicare which was sign into law by Former

President Lyndon Johnson. Medicare is medical insurance offered to people over 65 regardless of income or health.

My wife and I both have been using Medicare for over a decade. Without all of these programs I can't imagine how our lifestyle would change not only for my wife and I but for the whole country.

When I think of Thanksgiving I am reminded of a story I believe that displays a thanksgiving spirit.

There was a guy I had worked with more than thirty years ago. His name was Jordan Gayton. He always had a big smile on his face and was a friend to everyone.

Jordan had a warped sense of humor. He told me on one Thanksgiving Day he went for a walk in a valley behind the packing plant. There was some abandoned cars and a man living in one of them. Jordan said he talked to him and told him to wait right there and he would be back.

Jordan went home and made a big Thanksgiving plate and took it to him. He never thought much about it but it mattered to me.

Every Thanksgiving I would think about the kindness Jordan displayed towards a complete stranger. I believe people like him are born that way and think about people when others don't.

Jordon is gone now but his memory of kindness will always resurface in my mind during the Thanksgiving holiday season.

Chapter 40

Covid Plagued My Family

I usually write about Red Shirt Table where I grew up and the old stories my mother Lizzie Two Bulls-Swallow told me, but now I am writing about my battle with Covid 19.

Since March the country had cities on quarantine and the death rates were climbing. Eight months later here in Rapid City the numbers of Covid cases are consistently climbing.

My family and I let our guard down and all together stopped using hand sanitizer and disinfecting commonly touched surfaces. We did wear our masks out in public but that was not enough. My granddaughter and I got Covid.

It started Monday, November second. The wife and I pulled into our driveway. She got out of the truck and went into the house. I stepped down from the truck and I could feel my equilibrium was out of whack; I lost my balance and fell backwards.

Thankfully I didn't get hurt but I laid there for about twenty minutes because I couldn't get up off the ground. Finally my son Dale found me and helped me up. The next day I fell twice because of my equilibrium, once in the bedroom and the other in the living room.

My kids were concerned and had a family meeting. They banned me and the wife from going downstairs and going down our backyard hill. They said it was too dangerous.

On Wednesday the 4th I fell again in the living room and I couldn't get up. My grandson Nathan come and help me up.

My daughter Vikki got off of work early and took me up to Sioux San (hospital) to see why my equilibrium was off. Vikki and I were thinking what could be the reason why I was falling all the time and she suggested maybe a sinus infection because that will make your equilibrium off and I agreed.

At Sioux San they had me take a Covid test and it came back positive. I had no symptoms only sinus pressure and my equilibrium was off and I was extremely weak I needed to use a walker. My temperature was up a little but not a fever. I had no cough, nor sore throat, no head ache and no breathing problems.

They told my daughter to watch my temperature and oxygen level and if they get worse to take me to Monument Health (hospital).

Vikki called the house and let them know the test results and they began making me a bed in the living room away from my wife. Sioux San gave me a "Covid pack" with fever reducer, cough syrup, and sinus relief; then sent me home with Covid information.

That night Vikki spent hours sanitizing everything. I slept in the living room. I didn't feel sick—I just had sinus pressure and was weak. The next day went fine.

The wife stayed in her room and I stayed in the living room and only used one bathroom.

Our granddaughter, who lives with us, and our son Dale went in the afternoon and got tested for Covid and my granddaughter's test was positive.

Vikki got off of work early and took my temperature and oxygen level and my oxygen level was low. She said , "Dad I have to take you to Monument Health."

I had a men's Depends on and said I need to go to the bathroom and she helped me to the bathroom. I couldn't make it in time, I completely filled my depends.

My son Dale came and got me cleaned up and put on another Depends and we headed to the hospital. At the hospital, I was so weak I needed help from hospital staff to get out of the car and into the wheelchair. I ended up on the 10th floor. Every room had a door and all of the staff had protective gear on.

I didn't realize how serious I was until I seen the hospital staff quickly attend to me. The next day I thanked my daughter Vikki for making me go.

For a few days I didn't have any symptoms other than sinus pressure, being weak, and my oxygen level was really low.

About 5 days later I woke up one night and I couldn't breathe. I tried to take deep breaths but I couldn't seem to get enough oxygen. I called the nurse and they sat me up and increased my oxygen level on the machine and told me to breathe deep, it hurt the first few times.

The next day the doctors gave me two bags of platelets and it helped me. I then began doing breathing exercises to strengthen my lungs with two little plastic devices. One I breathe out and the other I breathe in.

During my stay at the hospital I can't count the times I peed on myself. The nurses cleaned me up every time and treated me with respect. One nice nurse said, "This is my job."

After a few more days the doctor said they want to wean me off of the high oxygen level on the machine so I can go home, but it will be a couple more days. I worked hard using those breathing devices to strengthen my lungs and the staff had me up and walking around.

Finally, on the eleventh day at the hospital the doctor said tomorrow you will get to go home. I was excited to get to go home. On the twelfth day I was still weak using a walker and on a lower level of oxygen, but I was finally home.

My sister-in-law, Susanna Swallow, sent some ox-tail soup and that was real a treat.

During my twelve day stay, the doctor kept close contact with my family giving them daily updates.

I want to thank Monument Health for their service to me and my family. They are all a blessing.

Although it never entered my mind that I might not come home, my family had a different view. The doctor made daily calls which set my family's mind at ease.

My first night home I was back in the living room isolated from my family because I was still contagious. The lights were out and everyone was in their beds. I cried. I cried real hard because I made it home.

I know three people who didn't make it home from Covid.

I want to thank several people who stepped up to help me and my family during this time. Thank you Susanna Swallow and her family for making soup, homemade bread and brownies. That food fed my family for a few days.

I also want to thank Wendy and Tonya Green who are my daughter Kate's childhood friends for making Indian tacos.

Thank you Cindy and Rob Schippacase for the soup and skillet bread.

I am grateful for my granddaughter Mandy for coming over often and cleaning my bed sore I got on my lower back. It is now completely healed.

I'm grateful for my daughter Kate who shopped for us and dropped off the groceries.

My son Dale cooked several meals for us and I appreciate that. I realize that I have a lot of people in my life who care about me and my family.

During that time we received many concerned calls, and people praying for us. I get a lump in my throat thinking about people who stepped up and expressed their concern. It reminds me of the goodness within this chaotic world.

It has been three weeks since I was released from the hospital and I am still struggling with breathing and on oxygen. The doctors say it will be awhile before I am off oxygen. I am slowing getting stronger every day. Now I can walk without a walker or cane, but I still get tired after being up and around the house.

Now I have a lot of time to think about how Covid effected me and my family. This pandemic is still new and not fully researched and everyday new things are being discovered. Several aspects keep running through my thoughts about what took place during this traumatic time.

What if we didn't have a "finger pulse oximeter" to read my oxygen levels? The wife is on oxygen and our granddaughter Mandy bought her one years ago, and my daughter Vikki used it to check my oxygen levels.

At that time I felt fine and had a fever of 101.5 but my oxygen was 86 percent. Might my story have turned out differently?

I also think about the severity of my wife being in the same house as my Covid positive granddaughter.

My daughter Vikki cleaned our house for hours everyday to prevent my wife from getting it. She did dozens of loads of washing from all of our bedding, towels and the blankets that cover our couches. All surfaces had to be cleaned several times a day and using hand sanitizer often. All towels were pulled daily and fresh one's put out.

Now we have bleach water made fresh every day and a hand sanitizer in every room. My daughter Vikki says we have to sanitize consistently and use sanitizer every time we are going to touch our face.

My family knows firsthand what it is like to experience the effects of Covid.

If you know anyone who is struggling with Covid reach out and help. There are several things you can do to help and still keep your distance.

1. Making meals not only helps the Covid positive people but the people taking care of them. My daughter said that the food that my sister-in-law Susanna dropped off was her saving grace because she didn't have time cook a meal to eat. Nothing like a home cooked meal to say you care.

2. Another way to help is with cleaning supplies; rags, bleach, Lysol, laundry detergent, reusable cleaning gloves, disposable masks, paper towels, just to name a few. Having the disinfecting products on hand is crucial to surviving Covid.

3. Grocery shopping is another way to help. The overwhelming aspect of disinfecting every household surface, doing laundry and feeding the Covid positive people is trying to fit in when to go shopping. You can get your list by phone or text and shop for them and when you deliver the groceries they can write a check for the groceries.

4. Running the families errands is another way to help. Cancelling appointments for the family and dropping off bills can help immensely. These are simple things that don't take long.

5. The last thing you can do to help is update the family and friends of the conditions the Covid positive people. When families are going through Covid, loved ones are constantly wanting to know updates. Getting a list of peoples' phone numbers and information on how they know the Covid people and their ability to text or only call is crucial. Then daily send out an individual text with the updates and make personal calls. This will take time but it's more time for the Covid positive care takers to take care of the sick people.

My daughter Vikki suggests not to send a group text to people to respect people's privacy. She says she texted one informational text with the updates of my progress and copied the texted and sent it to each individual separately.

Covid is going to be around for a while and we as a society have to take individual measures to form habits to stop the spread of this virus.

My family got a wakeup call and it could have costed me my life.

I look at life through grateful eyes and have a new attitude about what I can personally do to stop this pandemic.

Our elected officials failed us saying Covid was a hoax; Covid was concocted by the Democrats and the news media; and it would go away after the election.

Election is over and now our country has seen alarming numbers of Covid cases and depressing numbers of deaths. I won't waste a word on them who have no conscience, guilt or shame.

There is a strong wind coming that will clear out the infectious orange smog that is over our country and will let some sunlight in.

Sometime in the future there could be a parade with certain people on floats waving at the cheering crowd. You will see a tired old 81 year old Lakota man on the other side of the street with his back turned toward the parade proudly wearing his Native Veterans cap. That will be me.

Written by Victor Swallow and daughter Vikki

Chapter 41

Facts, Stories and Remembrance

I want to write about this COVID 19 and how it has affected me and my wife as Lakota senior citizens.

We both have health issues and our children are taking that seriously and making us stay home. We make a list of what we need from the stores and they shop for us a couple times a week.

When they come to the house, they are wearing masks. One of my daughters makes fresh bleach water since it is only good for 24 hours. Throughout the day, we wipe down with bleach water highly touched surfaces and wash our hands. We are taking measures to keep ourselves safe.

I realize more than ever that we are dependents now and grateful that our kids are stepping up to take the risks of going out to shop for us.

Since we have been at home with this social distancing in place, I have been on the phone reaching out to friends and relatives checking in on how they are doing. I also have been going for walks and doing more writing.

I want to share a story with you that has a little humor but it also touches the topic of no one should be forgotten. Every human life is precious and despite how people choose to live, life is still sacred.

Red Shirt Table people in early days did business in Buffalo or Fairburn mostly in Fairburn. I have heard my dad, John Swallow, talk about a store owner named C.B. Smith. The C for sure this was the team and wagon days.

My mother Lizzie Two Bulls talked about her brothers working in the Black Hills for a lumber company. She went along to help with the children. They also worked for someone in Buffalo Gap.

Her older brother, Stern Two Bulls, her mother said was drunk and tried to board a train and fell and lost three of his fingers. Uncle Stern loved his alcohol and he got drunk every chance he got which wasn't very often. Money was tight and sale to Indians was against the law.

I visited with his youngest daughter, Alice Merle Young, a few years back. She is gone now but I told her your dad was the nicest drunk I ever knew. When he was drunk he would sing Indian and laugh to himself.

I told her this story about her dad, he had a decent size log house about half-mile from my parent's house.

One day my brother said lets go to Uncle Stern's place and see if anybody is home. When we arrived there uncle was passed out on the west side of his house laying flat on his back with his moth wide open. A chicken was standing on his forehead pecking food out of his teeth. He didn't move a muscle.

After hearing the story Alice laughed and said that sounds like dad. Then she said one time her dad, who was a big man, came home drunk and opened a window and had a hard time crawling through the window. He found out later the door wasn't locked.

Alice told me she always wanted to get a grave marker for her dad but could never afford it. I went to the man who owned West River Masonry, a nice honorable man whose name is Steve Kroger. I told him I wanted to make a grave marker for my uncle. Steve said to go out in the yard and take whatever I wanted.

I took two wall cap-stones. I used a Dremel tool with a diamond bit and etched Stern Two Bulls January 18, 1891. When I told Alice she cried. When I got done I said to uncle's spirit, "Rest now, you're not forgotten." I imagine people walking by uncle's grave saying who is this Stern Two Bulls.

I know we are in a time of uncharted waters and the future is uncertain. This is a time to communicate with your loved ones and share some stories of your childhood memories and what your ancestors shared with you.

I know my kids have heard many of my stories numerous times but, out of respect, they humor me and listen to them again. I accept my family as they are, faults in all, and let them know that I love them unconditionally. Tell your family that they matter in your life and appreciate them!

Chapter 42

Looking Back on the Past Generations

I've wanted for many years to put my opinions in writing on religions, politics, and Lakota reservations. I've been able to look objectively at all three of them and nothing I see is good.

For this story I will go back two generations to my mother and grandmother's generation when Lakota women as a whole loved and nurtured their children and the men folk tried as best as they could to support their children.

During that time, the Lakotas in my family never knew why we lived on a reservation or how we got there. My generation served our country in great numbers for a country that did much evil to our people especially to my grandmother Mary Alice One Crow-Two Bull's generation.

She was born in 1871. Her father, One Crow, had two wives who were sisters, Rebecca and Fannie. Their parents were Fire Heart and Kind Heart and they were Hunkpapas. He had a child from each of his wives. My grandmother Mary's mother was Fannie. Rebecca had a girl named Nancy. Mom said they called Rebecca, Grandma Holy Day.

The government made my great Grandfather, One Crow, choose one of his two wives as his only wife. He chose Rebecca.

Fannie married Joe White Plume and had more children.

One Crow out lived Rebecca and married again and had a boy name Jim.

Grandma's generation was first introduced to processed foods and alcohol which would progressively ruin Lakota people over all the generations to this day.

Grandma was married to Fred Two Bulls who was three-quarter Lakota. She had eleven children that were born from 1891 to 1917, and 58 grandchildren who's blood degree ranged from five-eighth (5/8) to fifteen-sixteenth (15/16).

She loved each one of them equally even me, who was the craziest of the grandchildren.

Many of my grandmother's children died from eating a diet they were not used to eating and their bodies couldn't handle it.

Only five of her children lived to be in their eighties. Health problems and alcohol related incidents took many of the grandchildren.

There are thirteen grandchildren left, many of us with health issues and most of them know very little about grandma.

I have tried to imagine what went through my grandmothers mind when it came to religion.

Thinking about her own religious beliefs that sustained her people for hundreds of years to the new religion who God had a son who died, then back to life, and is somewhere in the sky, and someday will come again.

She also was taught to promise to swear allegiance to the Pope and would receive eternal life after death.

Most of this new religion could not have made any sense to her and yet through all the changes throughout her life and her people's she bore no hatred toward anyone.

She passed on at seventy-eight years old with a good heart she was honest and a very caring Lakota woman.

As I am writing this, I am so proud to be her grandson!

About the Author

Victor Swallow grew up in tents and cabins on Red Shirt Table, a small grassy mesa bordered by the non-vegetative Badlands National Park in southwest South Dakota. The nearest village, Red Shirt, isolated by the Cheyenne River, is in the far northwest corner of Pine Ridge Indian Reservation. Red Shirt currently has about fifteen dwellings, still no retail services, and is the poorest area in the U.S. His parents thought it was critical that Victor get educated like white people. He attended distance Indian boarding schools operated by the Presbyterian and Seventh Day Adventist churches. Following Lakota warrior tradition, Victor joined the U.S. Navy in the early years of the Vietnam War (1960-1964). After honorable discharge, he took any odd job a Lakotan could get to earn money—often working for area cattle ranches. In 1966 he became a construction laborer and eventually a life-member of the bricklayer's union while raising his family in Rapid City, SD with his wife, Melidie, who he lost during the Covid 19 pandemic. With sincere desire to pass on oral family stories, Victor hand-prints on notebook paper. With the help of his daughter, Vikki, some stories have been transcribed, typed, and included in this book, **Lakota Life After the Buffalo**.

Other GWW Books

Gary W. Wietgrefe books and e-books are sold by on-line retailers, New York distributor BCH at Ph. 914-835-0015, or signed by author ordered at RelatingToAncients.com.

www.ingramcontent.com/pod-product-compliance
Lightning Source LLC
Jackson TN
JSHW010830060525
83925JS00004B/20

* 9 7 9 8 9 8 8 1 7 3 6 7 0 *